THE STRATEGIC DIVORCE PROCESS

THE GUIDE TO DIVORCE, TAKE CONTROL AND PROTECT YOUR FUTURE

THE STRATEGIC DIVORCE PROCESS

THE GUIDE TO DIVORCE, TAKE CONTROL AND PROTECT YOUR FUTURE

MICHONE RIEWER

THE STRATEGIC DIVORCE PROCESS
© 2024 by Michone Riewer. All rights reserved.

Printed in the United States of America

Published by Igniting Souls
PO Box 43, Powell, OH 43065
IgnitingSouls.com

This book contains material protected under international and federal copyright laws and treaties. Any unauthorized reprint or use of this material is prohibited. No part of this book may be reproduced or transmitted in any form or by any means, electronic or mechanical, including photocopying, recording, or by any information storage and retrieval system, without express written permission from the author.

LCCN: 2024918082
Paperback ISBN: 978-1-63680-356-2
Hardcover ISBN: 978-1-63680-357-9
eBook ISBN: 978-1-63680-358-6

Available in paperback, hardcover, e-book, and audiobook.

Any Internet addresses (websites, blogs, etc.) and telephone numbers printed in this book are offered as a resource. They are not intended in any way to be or imply an endorsement by Igniting Souls, nor does Igniting Souls vouch for the content of these sites and numbers for the life of this book.

Some names and identifying details have been changed to protect the privacy of individuals.

Contents

Foreword 7
The Strategic Divorce Process 9
    The Limitations of Divorce Law 10
    The Different Kinds of Divorces 11
    Experience The Strategic Divorce Process 16
Step One: Decision-Making for the Children 21
    Medical Decision-Making 24
    Educational Decision-Making 25
    Religious Decision-Making 25
    Extracurricular Decision-Making...............26
Step Two: Visitation 29
Step Three: Child Support 41

Step Four: Maintenance 51
Step Five: Division of Assets and Debts 61
    Marital Debts................................62
    Marital Assets...............................64
    Categorizing the Assets 65
    Division of Assets and Debts 66
    Unequal Split of Assets 75
    Complexities during the Financial
    Discovery Process...........................76
Step Six: Pre-decree Litigation...................85
Life After Divorce..............................91
About the Author 99
About Strategic Divorce........................101

Foreword

Divorce is a journey often met with emotional turbulence, logistical challenges, and profound life adjustments. It is a process marked by both endings and new beginnings, where the landscape of one's life undergoes a profound transformation, and you have to make life-changing decisions.

In my many years of presiding over cases, I've witnessed countless divorce cases where it was apparent one of the parties wasn't prepared and "hoping for the best." Unfortunately, these types of cases don't lend well to hope alone.

The Strategic Divorce Process is a must-read for anyone entering a divorce. It's a beacon of guidance and support amidst the storm of dissolution. The book provides practical advice and resources to help individuals protect their interests and secure the best possible outcomes for themselves and their children throughout the complexities of divorce,

Foreword

allowing them to enter the proceedings with intentionality and foresight.

In these pages, you will find wisdom and practical strategies to navigate every facet of divorce, from legal proceedings and financial planning to co-parenting dynamics.

Knowing that divorce is not a one-size-fits-all experience, this guide offers a versatile toolkit that acknowledges the unique circumstances of each individual and family. The insights in this book will empower you to make informed decisions, foster resilience, and navigate through your divorce with confidence.

I commend you for embarking on this transformative journey with courage and determination. While the road ahead may be challenging, know that you are not alone. May this resource serve as an unwavering companion, illuminating the path toward a brighter tomorrow.

The Strategic Divorce Process

We've all heard the statistics, and because of that, we know that divorce is far from rare. With more than 50% of all marriages ending in divorce, everybody knows somebody (or several somebodies) who has gone through the process. Yet, for something so prevalent, most people entering a divorce know very little about how the process works until they're in it.

Very few people talk about their experience going through a divorce, and those who do often share unusual anecdotes or emotionally charged stories rather than facts about the process. Horror stories about what they may have lost in the proceedings, over-inflated tales of triumph, or advice from a divorce that took place decades ago are shared more often than real details that will help somebody understand what they can expect when going through a divorce.

The end of a marriage is a painful and often isolating experience, and while most couples know for a long time that their marriage is heading to its end, the process can feel so complicated and overwhelming that they put off filing and moving on for years on end.

While we can't remove the pain or hurt that comes from ending a marriage, we can help you better understand what the process is like—the limitations of divorce laws, the different types of divorce, and, most importantly, the Strategic Divorce process—removing much of the confusion and uncertainty that may be holding you back.

The Limitations of Divorce Law

When most people enter a divorce lawyer's office, they experience a wide range of emotions. They may feel broken, violated, lied to, betrayed, abused, or mistreated. They may feel embarrassed that they were unable to make their marriage work. They may feel like a failure or be grieving the life they previously had or had envisioned. They may feel completely numb to the process. They might even feel relieved.

All of these feelings are valid and perfectly normal, but they can also be incredibly destructive. Hurt feelings often cloud judgment, leading to unrealistic goals from the divorce, grounded not in a desire to win but to make sure their spouse loses.

Somebody may feel they are entitled to more than an even split—they may even be right. Unfortunately, the courts don't care. They aren't interested in why you believe you deserve more assets or money; they don't care how or why the marriage is ending, and it doesn't matter to them how hurt you may be. Courts are neutral. Illinois is a no-fault state, meaning that the courts follow the law without consideration of bad behavior either spouse may have engaged in. One spouse will not be entitled to or receive a larger share of the marital estate because their spouse had an affair, which led to the divorce.

While many people believe there is a great deal of wiggle room or that hiring a more aggressive lawyer and fighting for years will result in a better outcome, this simply isn't true in no-fault states. Divorce laws are strict and clear, and when it comes time for the judge to sign off on an agreement or rule after a trial, more often than not, these decisions are determined by a formula. This means the outcome is very predictable.

A good lawyer will help you understand your rights and represent your best interests so that you don't make any decisions that will have a negative impact on that formula, but they won't promise you something that isn't attainable or encourage you to fight your spouse to gain a split of assets that a judge would never order.

The Different Kinds of Divorces

When most people hear the word "divorce," they picture two parties at total odds with each other, slinging insults across a courtroom or fighting on opposite sides of a conference table. This is the perfect example of a contentious divorce.

Contentious divorces happen when parties let their hurt feelings or anger get in the way of rational decision-making. They may not know exactly what they want to get out of the divorce, but they do know that they want to hurt their spouse. They find themselves arguing over assets and decisions that don't matter rather than focusing on the big picture.

At Strategic Divorce, we encourage our clients to avoid a contentious divorce. We try to de-escalate the acrimony rather than fuel it. Unfortunately, not all lawyers share this sentiment.

There are lawyers who will take advantage of these destructive mindsets. Acrimony is their business plan, and it's easy to see what their intentions are.

When a client comes to them saying they want 70% of the marital assets, they don't explain why that won't be possible. Instead, they'll encourage their client to fight for 75%. The lawyer knows the limitations of the law. They know that a 75/25 division of assets is extremely unlikely and will result in a long-contested divorce. The lawyer also knows that the longer a divorce drags on, the more money they'll collect in legal fees.

Encouraging acrimony has a clear benefit for the lawyer and a clear drawback for the client.

On the complete opposite end of the spectrum is mediation. Mediation involves one mediator rather than two opposing lawyers. This mediator may be a lawyer who is well-versed in divorce law or an otherwise certified mediator. Their job is to help the parties come to an agreement that isn't necessarily based on what the courts would recommend but on what the two parties think is fair.

Of course, the judge still has the final say, and divorces that go through mediation have the same requirements as any other. Sometimes, the judge determines that the agreement favors one party too heavily and will refuse to sign off on it.

Mediation often works very well for everyone involved, but sometimes, it completely backfires. If the judge refuses to sign off on the divorce, one spouse may feel that the other tried to take advantage of them, and the one who was getting the more favorable deal will likely be less willing to compromise in the future. When this happens, we skip the possibility of an amicable divorce entirely and head straight for a contentious one.

Additionally, mediation can sometimes be used as part of an amicable divorce. If parties who are otherwise working well together are unable to agree on a specific part of the divorce, such as visitation, their lawyers will set up mediation. The parties will then meet with a neutral mediator to help them create a schedule that allows them to move forward.

The third kind of divorce, the one Strategic Divorce specializes in, is an amicable divorce. Much like mediation, the goal of an amicable divorce is to keep proceedings as civil as possible, focusing on what is realistic and coming to an agreement that both parties are comfortable with (or equally dislike). Unlike mediation, each spouse is represented separately by a lawyer.

This type of divorce can only be successful when the lawyers are realistic with their clients about what they can expect to receive. They encourage their client to think rationally, making decisions from a place of reason rather than allowing hurt feelings to run the show. This helps clients focus on what matters rather than wasting time (and money in legal fees) fighting over who gets to keep the air fryer (and yes, this does happen).

Of course, it's important that, even though the lawyer encourages amicability, they are capable of going to court. In fact, having a lawyer who is willing to fight for their clients and well-respected in the courtroom often helps the proceedings stay amicable.

If one lawyer knows the opposing lawyer is afraid or unwilling to go to court, they may leverage this to push for more favorable terms. If the case ultimately goes to court, the lawyer who rarely goes to trial may recommend that their client transition to a firm that is more experienced and respected in the courtroom. Firms like Strategic Divorce are then asked to step in, often long after the case has already begun, putting the client at a disadvantage.

However, if the opposing counsel understands that their opponent is a powerful trial lawyer and is willing to go to court, they may be more likely to settle the case amicably. Bullying or threatening their opponent with a trial is only effective if the opposing lawyer is not capable of going to trial. This is why the ideal lawyer is just as capable of defending and protecting their client's interests in a courtroom as they are when having a civil and productive conversation—and they push for the latter whenever possible. They know that when the divorce stays amicable, there are clear benefits for everyone involved.

First, financially speaking, it's much less expensive. The more time a lawyer spends on the case, the more money their client will need to pay them—and typically, these extra hours make very little, if any, difference to the end result.

For example, if one party fights for a 75/25 split of the marital assets, it's unlikely their spouse will agree to it, and the case will go to trial. The trial may end up costing around $100,000 in legal fees, and when all is said and done, the court will most likely equally divide the assets.

The end result from the case is the same: each party gets an equal share of the marital assets, but each spouse is walking away with less money than they would have had they skipped the trial altogether. For example, if the entire marital estate is worth $1,000,000 and the two parties proceed amicably and move through the divorce quickly, the total lawyers' fees may amount to $50,000. This leaves $950,000 to be divided, leaving each spouse with $475,000.

However, if the divorce becomes contentious, with one or both sides fighting for a large share of the estate, they may end up spending $300,000 (or more!) of the marital estate paying their lawyers, leaving $700,000 in the estate. It is unlikely that either party will achieve a drastically larger share, meaning both parties will walk away with around $350,000.

By choosing to fight for more than is reasonable or realistic under current divorce laws, each party will walk away with less money. Only the lawyers win in this scenario.

Amicable divorces are also much less emotionally expensive. While each party may still be hurt and angry about situations that led to the divorce, they're focusing their energy on moving forward rather than continuing to fight. If children are involved, this places a much lower emotional burden on them, as well.

Finally, amicable divorces take less time. A contentious divorce takes years to go to trial—years filled with uncertainty, anger, betrayal, and negative energy. And, as the acrimony never lets up or even continues to build, there is no opportunity to let those negative feelings go or begin to move on. It's a draining process.

At the end of a divorce, most people find that they aren't the same person they were when it started, just as they aren't the same person they were when the marriage began. When two parties work together to make the divorce as painless and easy as possible, it can be a catalyst for positive, intentional change.

However, when parties spend years fighting, it takes something out of them that they didn't intend to give. It's hard to move forward or even approach external situations with a positive mindset when you're expending so much negative energy on your divorce. People still find that they aren't the same person they were when the divorce started, but the change is much less likely to be as positive or intentional.

For all of these reasons and so many others, at Strategic Divorce, we strive to make every case an amicable one.

Experience The Strategic Divorce Process

When somebody first comes into the Strategic Divorce office, they'll meet with two lawyers to give their intake information. While most firms have one lawyer per client, we believe it's important to have two lawyers well-versed in the case. This way, if a question arises and one lawyer is in court or speaking with another client, there is another lawyer available who is knowledgeable about the intricacies of the case.

During the intake session, we start by hearing the client's story: we learn who they are, who their spouse is, if they have kids and how many, what their financial status is, what their home life is like, and so much more.

Next, and possibly most importantly, we figure out what has to happen for the client to feel like the divorce was successful. We want to know how they picture their life a year from that first meeting. What assets do they keep? What kind of child decision-making and visitation do they have? Where do they live? What job are they working? This helps us understand what matters most to our client and determine if their goals are attainable. We want to set expectations early so the client knows what limitations there are under the Illinois divorce laws. We gather enough information to ensure they get a fair and reasonable settlement focused on what matters most to them.

Then, once the client is ready, we move forward with the divorce or dissolution of marriage (which is the court's word for divorce). Every divorce starts with one party filing a Petition for Dissolution of Marriage, and the way this is done

The Strategic Divorce Process

sets the tone for the entire divorce proceeding. Typically, the spouse who is being served has no idea it is coming and is incredibly surprised when a sheriff shows up at their house or place of work.

Doesn't sound very amicable, does it?

When Strategic Divorce files a Petition for Dissolution, we try to avoid serving papers. Instead, we will send it directly to the other party via email. We include a letter that notifies them that we've been hired to represent their spouse and that their spouse has asked us to proceed amicably. It requests that they forward the petition to their lawyer and asks that they or their lawyer contact us within seven days so that we don't have to personally serve them.

We encourage clients to have a conversation with their spouse the day before they receive the paperwork. While most couples on the edge of divorce know it's coming, it still comes as a huge shock when proceedings actually begin. By warning the spouse the day before they receive the paperwork, we aim to dampen the initial shock.

That being said, we highly recommend that this happens after the papers are filed with the court and only a day before they receive the paperwork—not a month before—for a reason. The original petition is often written in a way that is slanted in favor of the filing party, so we want to make sure our clients file first. In addition, the filing party's lawyer gets to draft the final documents, which is another great reason to try to file first.

Getting to file first is a large advantage, as the lawyer of the spouse who files first drafts the final divorce documents. This enables the lawyer to use language they are comfortable with, likely slanting the final documents in their client's favor. Being the one to draft the final documents allows the lawyer to set the stage for the entire proceeding in a way that they believe will benefit their client and sets an amicable tone.

While the opposing lawyer will have the opportunity to make changes in an effort to ensure it is not favoring the party who filed, it takes significantly more time to do this, which costs the client more time (and money). Additionally, while the lawyer may catch some of the language that favors the party that filed first, it is possible that they won't catch it all and will be unable to add any language that slants the documents in their party's favor without the lawyer that filed seeing exactly what they changed.

After the petition has been sent, the spouse will either hire a lawyer or opt to represent themselves. (For the record, we recommend that you do not represent yourself—you want somebody on your side who fully understands the nuances of divorce law.)

The divorce process can feel very complicated, especially when first starting. In order to simplify it, The Strategic Divorce process breaks the divorce into five distinct sections if there are children involved and two if there are no children involved. We then guide our clients through the steps, one at a time. These steps are:

Step 1: Making decisions for your children. This covers how decisions for your children will be made, including what decisions can be made separately and which ones must be made jointly.

Step 2: Visitation. This outlines where the children will be sleeping every single day of the year.

Step 3: Child support. All cases with minor children must address child support.

Step 4: Maintenance. Often referred to as spousal support or alimony, there is a formula that determines whether or not one spouse should be required to financially support the other spouse.

Step 5: Division of marital assets and debts. This includes equitably (and often equally) dividing any property, debts, and assets you may have.

We'll also discuss the pre-decree litigation process. Because most divorces take several months, if not years, to finalize, there is usually a temporary order for visitation, child support, and maintenance before it is finalized in the judgment, which is the final document in the divorce.

Divorce is complicated. It can be messy. And when you're first starting out, it's incredibly overwhelming. From the time a couple first starts to consider divorce, it takes an average of two years before they actually meet with a lawyer, and it's easy to see why. It's hard to know what to expect if it's possible to emerge relatively unscathed or even where to start.

In this book, we'll break down the five areas that The Strategic Divorce Process will help you understand and resolve. We will explain each area in detail so you know what to expect at every stage. And with this knowledge of the process will come the strength and peace of mind to complete it.

STEP ONE

Decision-Making for the Children

Any divorce involving children includes discussions around decision-making and visitation, the two components that make up the custody agreement. Typically, decision-making for the children tends to be straightforward and uncomplicated, so it is usually determined first.

There are many decisions that come up throughout a child's life—from the big ones, such as where a child will go to school or if they'll have a medical procedure completed, to smaller ones, like what they will be eating for dinner each day. Generally speaking, the court tries very hard to keep most day-to-day decisions out of the custody agreement. What happens during each parent's visitation is their responsibility to handle as they see fit.

Decision-Making for the Children

However, for larger decisions, a decision-making structure is outlined. These decisions are separated into four categories: religion, education, medical, and extracurriculars.

There are three primary types of decision-making structures:

- sole decision-making
- sole decision with consulting
- joint decision-making

In sole decision-making, one parent gets the opportunity to make all of the decisions (in a given category) without the other parent having any input or approval. Typically, rather than having one parent in charge of all large decisions, each parent will have specific categories. For example, one parent will be in charge of medical decisions, and the other will handle all educational and religious decisions. Extracurriculars is the only category that is always joint, as there are financial implications for each parent.

This works very well in situations where the parents do not communicate well, there are abuse issues, or the parents aren't amicable, as it limits the number of interactions they may have or the number of items they'll need to agree upon.

However, sole decision-making structures are sometimes still utilized when the parents are amicable. One parent may feel more strongly about educational matters or understand that the other parent has knowledge that would make them better suited to make medical decisions, so they'll decide to divide the categories accordingly.

Additionally, if one of the parents is not as involved with the child's day-to-day life or lives far away, the parent with primary visitation will often have sole decision-making in each category, for simplicity's sake.

Still, most parents don't want to use a sole decision-making structure, as they feel strongly about being involved in all large decisions regarding their children. Many parents would be comfortable having sole decision-making power, but they are unwilling to give up their rights to make decisions in any category.

It is also possible to have sole decision-making with consulting. In this structure, the two parents are required to talk through any situation that arises together, trying to find a way forward that they can both agree upon. Of course, it is possible that the parents will not agree on every decision. Because of this, one party does still have the final decision-making power. However, they are required to consult the other parent and give them an opportunity to share their opinion on the matter.

If neither parent is willing to give up their ability to make decisions, they will often have joint decision-making. In joint decision-making, both parents have to agree on the decision being made, or neither party will get to make the final decision. If they are unable to come to an agreement, they will have to attend mediation in an attempt to find a solution. If mediation is unsuccessful, then either party can file a motion, and the court will make the decision for them.

While this may seem like a drastic solution, the vast majority of parents choose to move forward with joint decision-making, regardless of whether or not the relationship has remained amicable. Typically, neither parent wants to risk the other parent gaining sole decision-making power and agrees to joint decision-making as a compromise. While the involvement of mediation and potentially going to court may feel daunting, most parents find that they are able to agree on major decisions jointly without the need for mediation or court intervention.

If the two parents are able to agree on a decision-making structure, the courts will usually agree to what they have outlined. However, if they are unable to come to an agreement, the courts will typically give medical decision-making to one parent and educational decision-making to the other. This way, even if the parents are unable to work together, they each still have responsibility for one of the large categories of decisions.

Medical Decision-Making

The way sole decisions, with and without consulting, are made varies slightly in each category. For medical matters, there are three types of decisions: decisions in emergency situations, routine medical decisions, and non-routine medical decisions, as well as the choice of the medical provider.

In emergency situations, where decisions need to be made quickly, whichever parent has visitation at the time will make the decision on the spot, notifying the other parent as soon as it is possible.

For routine and non-routine medical decisions, one parent is usually responsible for scheduling all appointments. Routine medical decisions include matters like regular checkups, physicals, routine illnesses, and regular shots or vaccines. For these appointments, they get scheduled with notice to the other parent.

However, for non-routine situations, such as surgery, the parent in charge of scheduling the appointments is required to notify the other parent and make sure the other parent is available to attend if they want to. If the other parent must be consulted on the decision, the notification simply allows the other parent to be present, if desired, at the appointment. In joint decision-making, the parent is notified so that the two parties can come to an agreement on the course going forward. Of course, if they are unable to agree, mediation and court intervention will take place.

Educational Decision-Making

Educational decisions don't arise as regularly, as the decision-making structure only applies to major decisions, and not whether or not the student should do their homework or how they should study. These decisions include anything relating to special needs, such as an IEP, AP classes, and what school the student will go to, if there is an option.

Similar to medical decisions, a parent with sole decision-making power can make the decisions independently of the other parent. In sole decision-making with consulting, the parents will discuss the situation, but if they are unable to come to an agreement, the parent with the final decision-making power will determine what to do moving forward. In joint decision-making, the parties will discuss and need to agree on a course of action in order to move forward.

Religious Decision-Making

Religious decisions may be assigned to a parent, but they are typically very straightforward and are often outlined in the initial custody agreement without the need for an ongoing plan for decision-making.

This is largely because most parents will agree to continue to raise the children in the same religion they were raised in throughout the marriage. Even in mixed-religion families, religious decisions are rarely an issue, as the religion the children would be raised in was already determined when the children were very little.

It is typically outlined that the child will be raised in a specific faith and may attend services at a specific church where one or both parents go. That being said, neither parent is required to uphold any religious values or continue attending weekly religious services during their parenting time. It is solely meant to outline what each parent is able to do but does not force them to do it.

In rare cases where the parents cannot agree on what religion the children will be raised in or what religious services they may be allowed to attend, the courts will step in. While there is not a set precedent for how this is done, the judge will typically order that the children be taught about each parent's religious beliefs. Language included in the divorce decree will grant each parent the power to provide positive and meaningful religious experiences during their parenting time and be raised to understand and respect the faiths of both of their parents. This is done because the courts recognize that both religions are an important part of the children's culture.

Extracurricular Decision-Making

Finally, there are extracurricular decisions. Because both parents will be responsible for the time and financial commitments of extracurricular activities, they both have to agree to them.

Most activities that the child was involved in at the time of the divorce are automatically approved, while new activities or an increase in time or financial commitment to a prior activity will need to be discussed and agreed upon by both parties.

In extracurriculars, there is no sole decision-making, and one party cannot overrule the other. Instead, in the event that one parent wants the child to do an activity but the other doesn't, the child can usually still participate in the activity, as long as it only takes place during their visitation, and they agree to take full financial responsibility for it. Activities that are dangerous or include risk-taking are handled differently.

• • •

While there are several ways to approach decision-making, determining the best structure is typically very straightforward and helps reduce acrimony following the divorce. It allows each parent to proactively agree on many large decisions but also helps reduce the opportunities for contentious disagreements later on.

Once the decision-making structure is set, we move on to the second and vastly more complicated component of the custody agreement: visitation.

STEP TWO

Visitation

After determining the decision-making structure, we move on to the second part of the custody agreement: visitation. In the Strategic Divorce Process, we believe in outlining both parts of the custody agreement before any discussions regarding financials—whether it be child support, maintenance, or the division of assets and debts—take place.

There is a very good reason for this, specifically, that the courts want what is best for the children. While decision-making has no impact on the financial aspects of the divorce, the number of overnights each parent has is a driving factor in determining child support. Because of this, when children and financial issues are addressed at the same time, kids may be used as pawns for one parent to maintain more money. Alternatively, one parent may push for more parenting time than they really want in an effort to reduce their child support obligation. Neither of these things are in the children's best interests.

While the decision-making structure tends to be very straightforward, visitation is vastly more complicated. Between setting a standard weekly schedule, divvying up holidays, and scheduling vacation time, there are a lot of moving pieces, and all of them need to be outlined before the agreement can be filed.

Before any negotiations begin, we ask our clients what parenting time they want, as well as what they think their spouse will want. Will their spouse want a 50/50 schedule? Or will they prefer every other weekend and one night a week? Will they want any overnight stays at all or just daytime hours?

Some people may feel that a looser schedule is more appropriate for their families. They may have an amicable co-parenting relationship and believe a visitation agreement will be too constricting from the offset when they are more than capable of working together. However, the court will not accept any agreement that doesn't clearly outline where the children will be sleeping every single night of the year.

There has long been a perception that the court automatically grants women more favorable visitation—with good reason. Even as little as five years ago, courts generally saw women as the maternal primary caregivers. It was assumed that kids spent more time with their mothers, and because of this, the courts perpetuated this stereotype, giving the majority of the visitation to the mothers.

In many families, this led to a lot of conflict between children and their fathers. Kids would see their dad less than they did during the marriage and feel as though their dad deserted them or simply didn't care about being more present in their lives.

However, in the past five years, we've seen a huge shift in the division of parenting time. Thanks to discussions surrounding a father's rights, as well as how kids benefit from having both parents involved in their lives, fathers are no longer forced into a minor parenting role.

Today, 50/50 is the normal division of parenting time. For a judge to determine to award one parent more time, there needs to be concrete reasoning that one parent is less ideal such as a drinking problem, the parent not being home enough to reasonably care for their kids during the week, work hours that make transportation to and from school difficult, or a significant distance between houses.

There are several different ways that we can determine who has the children on each night with 50/50 visitation, but there are a few models that tend to be used most frequently. One that is commonly used, especially if the children are over thirteen years old, is one week on, one week off. The kids will spend one week, including the weekend, with parent A and transfer to parent B the following week, spending the week and weekend with them.

In other situations, a 5-2 schedule works better. For this model, each parent gets two set days a week, with the weekends alternating. For example, parent A has the kids Monday and Tuesday nights every week, while parent B has the kids Wednesday and Thursday nights. On parent A's weekend, they'll pick up the kids from school on Friday afternoon, and they'll stay with parent A until they are dropped off at school on Wednesday morning. Then, parent B will pick up the kids from school on Wednesday afternoon, and they'll stay with parent B until they are dropped off at school on Monday morning.

Similarly to one week on, one week off, each parent gets equal parenting time. These two models tend to work really

Visitation

well in situations where the parents do not have an amicable relationship, as all transfers happen at school, meaning the two parents do not need to see each other at all during the school year.

There are some other benefits to a 5-2 schedule, as well. First, many parents prefer this model because they don't have to go seven days without seeing their children on their off weeks. Additionally, there is added consistency with a 5-2 schedule as, aside from the weekends, the children are always at one parent's house on certain days of the week, and at the other parent's house on the other days. This makes it easier for both the children and the parents to schedule things, like doctor's appointments and playdates, and keep track of commitments, like extracurricular activities. Because of this, 5-2 is a popular schedule when parents have 50/50 visitation.

If the parents have equal time and they live in two different school districts, they can choose which to send their kids to, but if one parent has more overnights, even if it is just by a few days a year, their school district is the one the kids will attend.

While 50/50 visitation is attainable, some parents may make the decision that 50/50 is not in their child's best interest and opt to have less parenting time. For example, if one parent travels a lot for work during the week or works incredibly long days, making school pick-ups and drop-offs impossible, they may realize that a true 50/50 split just isn't realistic and is not in their child's best interest.

These parents may decide every other weekend visitation is in the best interests of their children. Others may opt to skip overnights altogether, preferring to spend a set number of waking hours with their kids during the week. This is used less commonly, as child support payments are based on the number of overnights per year, and by waiving all overnights, they are significantly increasing their child support obligations.

Still, when concerns about child support are taken out of the equation, these schedules can work well if the parents are capable of working together. Of course, there will be many more transfers than in the previously discussed schedules.

If the parents are at odds, however, this can be a breeding ground for parental alienation, and the increased contact caused by additional transfers can increase the opportunities for unpleasant behavior.

While many marriages end with hurt feelings, anger, and bitterness, most are able to shield their children from these feelings. They understand that having an amicable co-parenting relationship and fostering positive connections with both parents is in the best interests of their families.

However, in some cases, hurt feelings or a desire to reduce the child support obligation take over, and one parent actively tries to turn their kids against the other parent.

Some parents may try to alienate their children from the other parent because they hate the other parent and want the children to as well. Others realize that visitation will affect child support. They believe that by alienating their child from their spouse, the children will prefer staying with them, leading to more favorable visitation and child support obligations.

They'll do this in a variety of ways: criticizing their co-parent in front of the children, placing the blame for the relationship ending on their co-parent, or claiming the other parent doesn't see their children more because they don't want to.

While the alienating parent's goals may be to hurt their ex, hearing that "dad abandoned us for his new family" or "I guess mom is too busy for you" hurts the children more than

Visitation

anyone else. Regardless of whether the kids are toddlers or teenagers, if they are being consistently told that a parent doesn't care about them, they'll start to believe it. It won't just affect their relationship with the other parent; it will change the way they see themselves.

Parental alienation is an incredibly real problem. Severe alienation occurs in around 5% of cases, while some parental alienation likely occurs in as many as 30% of divorces with kids. Either way, it is hugely detrimental to children, destroying their self-esteem. So, why do the courts rarely acknowledge it?

The answer is simple: because they can't. A judge is very limited in what they can do, and while they can tell the alienating parent to stop, there is no way to monitor it, never mind enforce it. All they can really do is take some visitation away from the alienating parent in favor of the alienated parent. Most research shows that this isn't enough—unless all parental time is taken away, the bad-mouthing will continue, and the kids will continue to suffer.

If there is suspicion during the divorce proceedings that parental alienation may be happening, or if the parents are unable to come to a visitation agreement, a Guardian Ad Litem will be appointed by the court. A Guardian Ad Litem, or GAL, is a lawyer with specialized training who represents and is tasked with presenting the best interests of the children.

After being appointed, the GAL will meet with the mother, father, and other caretakers, such as grandparents, nannies, teachers, or other family members. They'll often meet with kids who are over four years old as well.

While what the kids say is taken into consideration, visitation isn't determined based on what the child wants, regardless of the child's age. Instead, the GAL is looking for red flags that would make one parent less suitable for equal or any visitation while filtering out any statements by the kids that seem like they were coached by one of the parents.

It's usually pretty easy to tell the difference. A coached child may say, "I only want to live with my daddy because I don't like my mom," while a child in real distress will reference real scenarios, like "When my daddy is angry, he throws things, and they break," or "Sometimes it's hard to wake my mommy up after she has a grown-up drink." Children who aren't coached are visibly affected by what they are saying, while children who are coached aren't.

In this way, the GAL serves as the eyes and ears of the court. After meeting with everybody, they'll work with the parents in an effort to help them come to a decision, and if they can't, they'll testify at trial so the judge can make a ruling.

In hotly-contested cases, one party will ask the court to appoint a custody evaluator. These psychological professionals will perform evaluations on both parents. They're looking to identify any issues that may be beyond the GAL's expertise, such as mental illness, drug abuse, or extreme alienation.

The court will almost always say yes to this request unless it is right before the trial. Similar to a GAL, this expert, referred to as a custody evaluator, will meet with the parties, the children, and other interested people and give their recommendations to the court. However, if one parent disagrees or doesn't trust that the recommendation will be fair, they have the right to obtain their own expert, which usually results in the second parent doing the same.

It's easy to see how the courtroom gets crowded in contentious divorces with complicated visitation concerns—each party's lawyer, a GAL, and three custody evaluators all work to provide the court with enough information to determine what is best for the children.

Visitation

Although anybody has the right to request a custody evaluator, they really should be reserved for abnormal circumstances rather than common disagreements such as dividing up holidays.

That's not to say that dividing up holidays doesn't get complicated and often very heated. Spending time with children when they are off of school and getting to celebrate special occasions is a hot-button issue for many couples. The easiest way to combat this is to divide holidays equally, usually rotating each year.

For example, if one parent has visitation on Thanksgiving during even number years, the other will get to celebrate Thanksgiving with their children on all odd number years. Holidays that take place over the course of multiple days, like Christmas, can be divided between the parents, alternating which parent gets each day every other year. If parent A has the kids on Christmas Eve on odd number years, they'll have Christmas day on even number years, and parent B will have the opposite schedule.

Because children are also on school vacation over the winter holidays, the visitation schedule for the two-week break often varies from their traditional structure, ensuring each parent gets equal time with the kids and gets to celebrate both Christmas and the New Year with them. Parent A will have the kids for the first week, but parent B will get one day in the middle—either Christmas or Christmas Eve—while parent B will have visitation during the second week, with parent A getting one day in the middle, either New Year's Eve or New Year's Day.

Parents who are committed to remaining amicable even after their divorce may try to simplify things by claiming they'll all spend Christmas together—something we strongly recommend against putting in the visitation agreement.

While we hope the relationship stays amicable in the years to come, as the parents move on from the marriage and possibly remarry, shared holidays may become awkward or simply may not be feasible. Instead, we recommend having holidays allocated separately, knowing that each parent can invite the other whenever they choose to.

If it seems like there are extensive precedents set around Christmas, it's because there are. With so many traditions surrounding the holiday, it's one that is incredibly important to most families, even if they aren't Christian.

Holidays that extend the weekend, such as Memorial Day or Labor Day, need guidelines as well. Every visitation agreement needs to determine if these holidays should only account for the extra day or the entire long weekend they fall under.

When one of the parents lives in another state, they are often allocated more time during holidays and summer vacations.

After reading all of this, it should come as no surprise that holidays take a long time to determine—usually longer than anything else except daily visitation.

While the visitation allocation should remove any uncertainty or questions surrounding who has the children on any given day of the year, there are situations where the agreement may need to change even after the divorce is complete.

One of them is relocation. Once a divorce is finalized, any parent who has the majority of the parenting time or intends to keep equal parenting time is not allowed to move more than 25 miles from the marital residence without obtaining permission from their ex-spouse or the court. If one parent agrees to the other parent's move, they are able to formalize it quite easily. However, if the parent does not agree, the moving parent will have to file a motion to allow relocation. It is not easy to have this approved: a very high standard has to be met to prove that the children will benefit from the move.

If the parent who is moving does not have primary visitation or does not feel strongly about retaining 50/50 visitation, they are able to move without getting any kind of permission. The visitation schedule and child support obligation may need to change accordingly, with any and all travel costs their sole responsibility.

Relocation is a situation that may never apply to any given divorce. However, one situation that likely will is the right to first refusal.

If one of the parents needs to be away from their children during their visitation, the other parent gets to decide if they want to have extra visitation during that time before any alternate childcare is arranged. For example, if parent A has to go away for a weekend when they normally have visitation, they have to ask if the other parent wants to have the extra time with their children before arranging any alternate childcare, like a step or grandparent.

The amount of time a parent needs to be away from home for this to be triggered varies on a case-by-case basis. It may be only 4 or 6 hours with younger kids, while it's often overnight with older children.

Outlining visitation is a complicated and usually very long process. It often takes longer than all other aspects of the divorce combined. However, once it is outlined, it gives each parent a clear roadmap moving forward.

After the divorce is complete, most parents, especially those who part amicably, understand what the agreement is and put it in a drawer somewhere in their home so that they can easily access it when they need to reference something, like what year they have their kids for Memorial Day.

The Strategic Divorce Process

These couples are often more willing to work together flexibly, as well. They understand that life can be unpredictable (especially life with kids!) and are willing to trade days or make changes as needed.

Of course, not everybody shares this sentiment. Sometimes, specifically in more contentious divorces, couples will stick to the letter of the agreement down to the minute, often hoping to catch their former spouse making a mistake. As with parental alienation, the children tend to be affected most of all.

• • •

Once the custody agreement, containing both the decision-making structure and the visitation schedule, is in place, it doesn't tend to change much in the years that follow the divorce. If, for some reason, a change needs to be made, the parents need to work together to come to an agreement or attend mediation before involving the court.

If both parents are on the same page, they can simply come to an agreement, memorialize the agreement in an order, and file it with the court. If the parents are not in agreement, they are required to see a mediator in an attempt to find a solution before going to court. Going to court to make a change is always the last resort.

The only exceptions to the requirement to mediate before approaching the court are cases where the physical safety of the children may be at risk, such as abuse, drug use, or neglect.

The custody agreement is a long, often complicated, and frequently emotionally exhausting process. But it's usually the hardest part of the divorce, and once it is complete, the next three steps move much more quickly.

STEP THREE

Child Support

After the custody agreement has been reached and the allocation judgment has been entered as a final order by the court, we move on to the marital settlement agreement. In this next stage of The Strategic Divorce Process, we determine how assets and debts will be divided, whether and how much maintenance (also known as spousal support or alimony) will be paid each month, how much child support will be paid, and to whom.

As part of The Strategic Divorce Process, discussions around child support only begin once the custody agreement has been reached and with good reason. While the decision-making structure has no effect on child support, the visitation schedule is a large driving factor in the amount of money one spouse will pay, so it must be determined first.

Child Support

Child support is an obligation of both parents to support their child until they are 18 years old or have completed high school, whichever comes second. Typically, one parent will pay the other a set amount of money each month to help with living expenses for the child. The right to child support support cannot be waived permanently by the parent receiving the money, as the money isn't intended to be used for them but for their kid's well-being. Unlike maintenance payments, child support is the right of the child.

While many people think it's possible to negotiate the dollar amount of child support, that just isn't the case. Child support is not calculated based on wrongdoings or perceived faults during the marriage or divorce; it's not even determined by a judge. Child support is calculated with a math equation, plain and simple.

Well, the concept may be simple, but the equation certainly isn't. This complicated equation takes a variety of variables into account when calculating how much child support will be owed. While some are obvious, such as the number of overnights and each parent's income, others, such as who pays health insurance, are less obvious, and many parents may not have thought to consider them.

In addition to child support payments, parents usually divide the cost of additional expenses proportionate to their income. These expenses can include school fees, medical costs not covered by insurance, extracurricular activities, and other costs that don't fall under day-to-day expenses. Often, there is a 40/60 split, with the parent who has the higher income paying 60%, regardless of the visitation schedule.

Child support is calculated separately. Rather than covering the infrequent expenses, this is meant to help with everyday costs that parents incur during their visitation, like clothing, housing, food, and day-to-day living.

The first step in determining the amount of child support is knowing who will be receiving it. If one parent has over 60% of the overnights, the other parent will likely owe them child support even if the parent with more visitation has a higher income.

Parents who have less than 40% of the overnight visits will pay significantly more child support than those who have more than 40%, even if the difference is only a few days. For example, parent A and parent B split visitation evenly. Parent A has a higher income, and the equation determines that Parent A owes $500 a month for both children. If parent A reduces their visitation slightly, the child support will likely remain the same. However, if their visitation drops below 40% or less than 145 nights per year, the amount they are paying will likely double.

Whoever has greater visitation is significant in other ways as well, as this parent will likely get the tax benefit from each child. The tax filing status of each parent is also taken into the child support equation.

This may seem like an insignificant thing to consider, but it can have a large effect on the parent's net income, and net income, not gross income, is what child support is based on. State and government taxes reduce each parent's gross income, so their filing status will help determine what their net income really is. However, other payments that come directly out of the paycheck, such as HSA or retirement contributions, are not deducted from the net income.

Maintenance payments can also affect the amount of child support. Although they are calculated separately, maintenance is considered income for the parent receiving it, which will reduce the income gap between each parent, affecting the child support calculation.

For example, if one parent makes a net income of $3,000 a month, but their maintenance is $4,000 a month, their income would be $7,000 a month. If their spouse's net income is $13,000 a month and pays $4,000 a month in maintenance, their net income would now be calculated at $9,000 a month. For calculating child support and the proportionate division of the child's expenses, this brings their monthly income gap to $2,000 rather than $10,000.

In situations where the higher-earning parent has over 60% visitation, child support payments may offset the amount of maintenance they will owe their spouse. For example, parent A has 65% of the parenting time, meaning parent B has to pay child support, which has been determined to be $1,000 each month. However, parent B makes significantly less money than parent A. Because of this, parent A owes $3,000 in maintenance each month. Rather than exchanging checks, the child support is deducted from the maintenance, meaning parent A now pays $2,000 in maintenance rather than the full $3,000. This is possible because the tax consequence of each type of support is the same.

Because the length of the marriage heavily determines the duration of maintenance payments, maintenance payments may not continue until the children are 18 years old or finish high school. In these cases, after maintenance payments have ceased, child support is recalculated. For example, Parent A and Parent B were married for five years, which typically means maintenance payments will take place for a year. However, they have a child who is three years old, meaning child support will continue for 15 years. While maintenance payments are being made, they are factored into the income of each parent, affecting the child support calculation. Once maintenance ends, the parties will have to recalculate child support and the division of expenses accordingly.

While child support typically ceases once the child turns 18 or graduates high school (whichever comes second), there are some situations that would cause child support to continue. Section 513 of the Marriage and Dissolution of Marriage Act provides for the educational expenses of a non-minor child and a non-minor child with a disability.

Unlike married parents, who have no obligation to pay for their kids' college, divorced parents do. There are a few different ways the obligation is calculated, but for each one, the cost of college is based on the current estimated in-state expenses, including tuition, room and board, books, and other supplies to the University of Illinois. This amount can be found on the University of Illinois website and updates annually, and if the divorce agreement is written correctly, the amount each parent is responsible for will adjust accordingly, as well. If the child decides to go to a college that will cost more, the parents are not legally responsible for paying any amount over the in-state tuition.

The first and most common model for dividing up the cost of college is proportionate to each parent's income and their ability to pay. Unlike child support payments, which only take into account each parent's income, the calculation of contribution to college is based on the household's income. For example, if a stepparent makes seven figures a year, this is not accounted for in child support, but it is considered when determining college payments.

Sometimes, the child may be responsible for a third of the payments, be required to do a work-study program, and/or have grants or loans in their name to apply to their portion of the payments.

If this seems much more flexible than child support payments, that's because it is. There isn't a strict formula for funding college, so there is a lot more wiggle room, leaving it

Child Support

open to the judge's interpretation. Judges can say the parents have no obligation, but this is incredibly rare.

If the court determines that the parents have an obligation, there are requirements for the student. The student can only go to school under this agreement for four years and must be a full-time student. They also have to give their parents full access to school information, such as financial aid information and their grades, and must maintain at least a C average. Additionally, the student must begin college within a year of graduating high school, barring any medical or mental health complications that justify a delay, or the parents will no longer have any obligation.

Aside from college, the statute also covers support for a non-minor child with a disability. If a child is disabled, one parent can apply for support, much like with a minor child. However, this support often causes some problems with social security disability benefits, which the child or their guardian may be entitled to after 18 years of age. The federal government has determined that these social security benefits should be sufficient to care for the adult child, and therefore, the state court hearing the divorce matter often agrees that additional child support may not be needed.

After the divorce is finalized and child support has been fully outlined, parents have the right to approach the court if there is a substantial change of circumstances that they believe will impact their obligation. In these cases, the parent who believes they should receive additional child support or lower the amount they currently pay can file a motion to modify child support (as well as maintenance, if applicable) based on a substantial change of circumstances.

One reason the amount of child support may change is maintenance ends. In this situation, the party who loses maintenance can file, as it may greatly reduce their monthly income, increasing the other parent's child support obligation.

Another example is a parent getting a substantial raise at work or having a decrease in income. In these situations, the law is relative. If both parents have received a similar percentage increase or decrease in income, it likely would not be significant enough to be considered a substantial change.

There are, of course, some people who may try to take advantage of this.

On July 1, 2017, the way child support was calculated in Illinois changed drastically.

Before July 1, 2017, the non-custodial parent paid a percentage of their net income based on the number of children. However, the new law uses an income shares approach where the divorce court is required to order an amount of money that would be allocated for the care of a child based on the combined income of the parents, as well as living expenses, the number of children, the number of overnights the children spend with each parent, health insurance costs, and a plethora of other factors.

Previously, any parent who had less than a true 50% of parenting time paid child support, regardless of whether it was over 40% or as little as no overnight visits. Now, the amount changes drastically at the 40% mark. For parents who have overnights 41-49% of the time, this changes their obligation significantly.

This change in child support law by itself is not enough to file a motion to modify support. The law requires you to prove a Substantial Change of Circumstance, but if there is any change, even one that seems as though it may raise the child support obligation (such as a large raise), a motion can be filed to modify the support. If the support was originally calculated prior to July 1, 2017, it will most likely result in a lower monthly payment moving forward.

For example, prior to 2017, if parent A had the children overnight on 182 nights a year and parent B had the children overnight on 183 nights a year, parent B would be considered to have primary visitation, even though it is as close to 50/50 as possible. If both parents had the same income of $300,000 a year, parent A would have owed parent B $4,717 each month.

However, after the equation changed in 2017, the same circumstances would result in parent A owing parent B $26 a month, as parent B only has one extra overnight each year.

This, of course, changes depending on the income of each parent. Prior to 2017, with the same overnight schedule, if parent A earns $300,000 a year, but parent B doesn't have any income, parent A would still owe $4,717 each month. However, in the years that followed 2017, child support would be set at $2,649 each month.

Because of the substantial difference, parties who become aware of this law are often very eager to find any possible substantial change. Not only will they report a raise, but they'll willingly take a pay cut, knowing they could end up with more income each month once they are paying less in child support.

In amicable divorces, this rarely happens. Most parents only care about what is best for their children, and as long as there are no financial concerns, they are happy to keep paying their child support, knowing it will be used for the children's benefit.

The higher earner may even receive a raise and contact their lawyer, believing their obligation should be higher, but choose not to move forward with filing once they realize their obligation will actually decrease.

In this way, there are added financial benefits to remaining amicable during and after the divorce. Returning to court is expensive, both in time and in lawyer's fees.

Aside from changes in income, changes in visitation can be considered a substantial change of circumstances. Changes in visitation can be made verbally and do not need to be put in writing or documented in a court order. If an oral agreement is made, this will have no impact on child support payments. However, if the visitation is changed in court, and it is substantial, then the payor could file a motion to modify child support, and it will often be recalculated.

Even parents who co-parent very amicably can find themselves in a tight spot here. One parent may ask the other to take on an extra day a week due to work or personal obligations. Suddenly, one day turns into two, which turns into three, and one parent has the children all but one day a week.

Often, they're happy—they wanted more time with their children all along, and now they have what they wanted. But they also may be frustrated that their ex-spouse fought for 50/50 visitation to avoid paying child support, only to drop well below the 40% threshold, meaning, if their case was finalized after 2017, they are paying much less child support than they should be or even receiving money that they aren't entitled to.

At this point, they may go to their lawyer to see if they can get the visitation schedule formally revised. Either way, it's important to consult a lawyer so the correct strategy can be considered. We always recommend that our clients exercise caution in these situations. It's possible that the other parent will claim the changes in visitation were only temporary due to a family emergency or outlying work problem, and the judge will leave the agreement as is.

Now, the other parent will likely stick to the letter of the agreement, taking back all of the visitation they originally had bestowed upon the other parent.

Because of this, if the most important thing to the client is having as much time with their children as possible, it may not be worth taking the risk to get the visitation agreement formally revised. Most people can't quantify the possibility of losing time with their children unless they are struggling financially, so they often choose not to file.

However, parents who have a contentious divorce or a bad co-parenting relationship will almost always go back to court. The parent who has taken on more visitation than outlined may be (rightfully) upset that their ex-spouse fought for 50% of the overnights, knowing they only really wanted 20%, just to get out of paying as much, or any, child support.

Any change to the child support agreement must be in writing and solidified in a court order. Proof of an agreement through email, or even a written and signed agreement, will not be honored by the court. This can be confusing, as visitation can and is often changed verbally, but money cannot be. Ex-spouses may verbally decide to change the child support obligation from $500 to $250 every month, but unless that has been outlined in a court order, the person paying child support still owes the other parent half of their payment each month, and it will add up quickly. If something changes and it is brought to court, that parent will be responsible for the entire difference as a lump sum.

• • •

While many of the decisions that factor into child support may be complicated, the actual equation leaves very little room for interpretation. Once the custody agreement has been reached, child support is a pretty quick discussion, and when parents work together, realizing that they both want what is best for their kids, it tends to be even easier.

STEP FOUR

Maintenance

Whether you know it as alimony, spousal support, or maintenance, we're all talking about the same concept—and it's one that is important to understand, considering it's something that comes into play in many divorces. It's also the next step of The Strategic Divorce Process.

There have long been misconceptions about what maintenance is, how it is calculated or determined, and who is entitled to it, and we're going to take the opportunity to clear those misconceptions up.

Simply put, maintenance is supplemental income paid from one spouse to the other after their divorce. The purpose of this income is to allow both spouses to live the same lifestyle they were accustomed to during their marriage.

Of course, this optimistic view isn't entirely realistic. The reality is that when two people divorce, even though their

Maintenance

combined income will likely stay the same, their expenses are usually nearly doubling, as the income is now being divided between two separate households with separate rent or mortgages, utility bills, and other costs.

The courts use maintenance to ensure that both parties have enough money to survive comfortably, rather than one party thriving while the other may be struggling to get by or forced to make extreme lifestyle changes.

When determining who will pay maintenance, the primary factor is income. The lower wage earner will always be the one to receive maintenance, and any and all reliable sources of income, not necessarily just employment, should be identified and used in the calculation. This can include regular family gifts, investments that have regular returns, perks from employment, such as car allowance or cell phone contributions, or cash from hobbies or side projects. Essentially, this is any income that can be claimed on a tax return, in addition to other reliable sources of money.

One of the biggest misconceptions about maintenance is that it is entirely at the court's discretion. The reason for this misconception is obvious; up until 2016, that *was* the case. Courts were asked to determine maintenance not only on the income of each spouse but also based on their lifestyle with wide latitude.

Courts would assess each party's salary, the lifestyle of the couple, anything that may have negatively affected one spouse's earning potential (such as putting their career on hold to raise children), how much the couple had saved, and how the family's money was being spent.

In order to prove why their client needed substantial maintenance or why their client should pay less maintenance, lawyers were forced to provide extensive details about their client's lifestyle. Divorces dragged on for years as lifestyle was proven, and it was nearly impossible to keep relationships amicable when lawyers and the courts scrutinized every financial decision.

Then, in 2016, in Illinois, the equation to determine maintenance was created, and it revolutionized family law. No longer was maintenance determined by the presiding judge, and lifestyle became irrelevant for families with a combined income of less than $250,000. In 2019, that income threshold was changed to $500,000. For most people, maintenance, much like child support, is now determined by a formula applied by the courts.

Turning maintenance into a math equation sped up divorces considerably while decreasing acrimony between the two parties, as arguing was unlikely to make a financial difference in either direction.

From 2016 to 2019, the formula was 30% of the higher wage earner's gross income minus 20% of the lower wage earner's gross income. However, at that time, maintenance was taxable. This meant that the higher wage earner was able to deduct the amount of maintenance they were paying from their income, often putting them in a lower tax bracket, allowing them to pay taxes at a lower percentage.

Meanwhile, the person receiving maintenance was not getting enough money to move up a tax bracket and typically was taxed at the same percentage that they would have been without maintenance.

The IRS was losing tax money, and because of this, they changed the equation. Any divorce that was completed prior to 2019 was able to keep using the old formula, and maintenance remained a federal income tax deduction, even if the amount of maintenance being paid changed. However, for all new divorces taking place in or after 2019, a new formula was used.

Maintenance

Currently, the formula is:

33% of the higher wager earner's net income − 25% of the lower wage earner's net income = annual maintenance paid.

There are some exceptions to this equation. First, the amount of money the lower wage earner receives in maintenance cannot exceed more than 40% of the couple's combined net income. If the amount calculated by the standard equation does exceed this amount, 40% of the combined net income is used instead as a cap.

Additionally, should the couple's combined gross income be in excess of $500,000 annually, any maintenance awarded on income in excess of $500,000 can be calculated differently at the judge's discretion.

In Illinois, judges have interpreted this statute to mean that the first $500,000 of income is calculated using the standard equation. However, any income in excess of that is calculated as the judge sees fit. In these situations, the judge may choose to use the same equation for all income. Alternatively, they may opt to calculate any additional income in excess of $500,000 differently, awarding the lower wage earner a different percentage of the income or adopting a tiered approach.

In a tiered approach, the maintenance percentage is calculated differently at different dollar amounts. For example, the first $500,000 is calculated using the standard equation. The judge may decide that the next $250,000 of income is subject to 20% maintenance, and any income in excess of that will have maintenance calculated at 10%.

For spouses who do not work outside the home and do not have their own income, such as a stay-at-home parent, an imputed income is often entered into the equation to represent their earning potential rather than their actual income.

This adjustment reduces the maintenance obligation for the higher earner.

While temporary maintenance may begin during the divorce, standard maintenance payments begin monthly once the divorce is completed, but, in most cases, they do not go on indefinitely. There are a few different ways the maintenance obligation can end.

The first, and likely most obvious, is time. The length of the maintenance obligation is primarily determined by the length of the marriage, with longer marriages having a longer maintenance period.

Much like the amount of maintenance paid is determined by an equation, how long maintenance will continue has its own formula. In Illinois, maintenance lasts a certain percentage of the time the couple was married, with the percentage getting larger the longer the marriage lasted. Every year over 5 years has a specific percentage assigned to it.

For example, if the couple was married for less than 5 years, the maintenance period is 20% of the length of the marriage. If the couple was married between 10 and 11 years, the maintenance period is 44% of the length of the marriage. For couples married 15 to 16 years, the maintenance period is 64% of the length of the marriage, and if the couple was married for more than 20 years, the court will order maintenance for a period of time that is either equal to the length of the marriage, or indefinitely. For marriages under 10 years, maintenance usually terminates once the allotted amount of time is up.

A common way that maintenance ceases, aside from the clock running out, is if the payee gets remarried or cohabitates with a romantic partner. In cases of cohabitation and not marriage, it needs to be proven that the payee is living with a romantic partner on a continuing and conjugal basis.

Maintenance

Some judges will require proof that the couple is co-mingling some of their funds or ask for proof that the relationship is serious, like photographs taken at a family event.

Maintenance also ceases if either of the spouses passes away. In some cases, the court or the parties will decide that maintenance should be secured by life insurance, which will be outlined in the marital settlement agreement. In these cases, the spouse paying maintenance is required to cooperate with securing life insurance, but the person receiving life insurance may be responsible for paying the premiums unless the parties agree otherwise. This ensures that if the payor passes away, the payee will still receive some financial assistance.

While the amount and length of time of maintenance is determined by a formula, a different structure can be negotiated, if both parties are open to it.

One spouse may agree to a higher amount of maintenance to be paid over less time, or one spouse may waive maintenance entirely for a larger share of the marital estate.

This may be done for a variety of reasons, such as the person receiving maintenance knowing they'll get remarried quickly, cutting short the amount of time they'll receive payments anyways, or a payor who is looking to retire and does not want to continue the maintenance obligation throughout retirement.

Oftentimes, the amount or length of maintenance is used to offset assets that cannot be split equally. For example, if the couple has two assets with different values—such as a home valued at $500,000 and a business valued at $1,000,000—they may choose to increase or decrease the maintenance amount, rather than attempt to split both assets equally.

As long as the parties' agreement regarding the division of assets and the setting of maintenance feels fair and equitable, it does not need to remain consistent with the traditional formula. However, if the judge thinks the split is unconscionable (extremely unfair), they will not sign off on it. The courts do this so that one party isn't bullied into accepting terms that aren't fair to them or have any ignorance of their rights taken advantage of.

However, if the two lawyers who helped the parties come to the agreement are available to answer the judge's questions and explain why the untraditional split is equitable, the judge will likely allow it.

A lawyer will also ensure that the marital settlement agreement is drafted to protect their client if there is a substantial change of circumstances. Much like child support, the amount of maintenance can be changed if there is a substantial change in circumstances for either of the parties.

While many events may be considered substantial changes in circumstances, there aren't necessarily set precedents that define how those changes are handled. Because of this, it's important that the marital settlement agreement thoroughly outlines any change in circumstances that is likely to occur.

A common event is the payor retiring from their job—an event that will significantly change their income. However, a planned retirement may not be considered a change in circumstances unless it is outlined as one in the marital settlement agreement. This means that while the payor's income may change significantly, their maintenance obligation may not. Because of this, having a lawyer who is familiar with how retirement affects maintenance is important.

Other changes that will affect the maintenance amount can include job loss, income reduction due to no fault of their own (such as pandemic-related pay cuts or layoffs related to the economy), or a substantial increase in income (over 10%).

Maintenance

In the cases of substantial increases in income, there is usually a cap, and any income over that amount won't raise the maintenance. This cap is typically the highest wage the payor earned during the marriage. It is important to negotiate a cap on maintenance during the divorce negotiations. A cap on maintenance is used for two reasons.

First, the purpose of maintenance is to allow each spouse to maintain the lifestyle they had during the marriage. If the payor experiences a windfall, like their salary going from $200,000 annually to $500,000 annually, increasing the maintenance would go far past maintaining the lifestyle of their former spouse.

Child support, however, will increase accordingly, as the courts believe children are entitled to benefit from any circumstances their parents benefit from. So, while maintenance will not be raised by a windfall, child support will.

Setting the maximum income amount for purposes of calculating maintenance as the highest wage the payor earned during the marriage also protects the payee. Many people lose their jobs or end up having a decrease in salary right before a divorce takes place. Sometimes, the financial stress of income loss is a contributing factor in the divorce. Other times, the job loss or income decrease seems to be an intentional ploy to reduce the amount of maintenance or child support. By capping the amount of maintenance at the highest income the payor received during the marriage, the payor's maintenance will increase if or when their salary increases again.

In cases of job loss or medical issues that may have halted or significantly reduced income, the courts may decide to reserve maintenance. This means that, while maintenance is not appropriate in the current financial situation, it likely will be one day, so maintenance will resume or begin once it makes sense.

In cases where the primary earner appears to lose their job purposely, be purposefully underpaid, or it seems they may underreport their income, the judge may give a disproportional share of the marital estate to the other spouse in lieu of maintenance. Alternatively, the judge may assign an income representative of the spouse's actual earning ability. The court tries to make it fair.

• • •

Despite how clearly maintenance is outlined under Illinois law, there are some divorces that are immune to any laws surrounding maintenance payments because they have pre-nuptial agreements. A pre-nuptial agreement is a contract that sets the terms of the divorce prior to the marriage taking place and supersedes Illinois divorce laws. Assuming the contract is valid, whatever is outlined in the agreement will be followed.

If the pre-nuptial agreement says there will be no maintenance in the event of a divorce, there will be no maintenance. If the agreement specifies a different formula for the calculation of maintenance or the amount of time maintenance will continue, that will be followed as well.

A valid pre-nuptial agreement does not expire, and will be upheld. However, if the pre-nuptial agreement was signed under duress, it will likely be considered invalid. This may be the case if one party was given the pre-nuptial agreement a few hours before the wedding and told to sign it, or the wedding will be called off, or if a party was coerced into signing it.

Maintenance

However, if both parties had time to review the contract and were able to have a lawyer review it to protect their interests, it would likely be considered valid, even if one party had significantly more bargaining power than the other, as the spouse with less bargaining power was not forced to get married.

Pre-nuptial agreements very rarely come into play during divorces—less than 5% of all divorces involve pre-nuptial agreements. Because they are uncommon, most divorce lawyers don't ask their clients if they have one at the beginning of divorce proceedings, which is why it is vital that clients inform their lawyer if they have one immediately. If a pre-nuptial agreement is in place, there may not be any room to negotiate, and knowing this will save time and money for all parties.

• • •

Generally speaking, maintenance, like child support, is fairly straightforward. Unless one of the parties wants to bargain or negotiate, the standard maintenance equation will drive the discussion, helping to avoid any contention or acrimony. If the parties do want to negotiate, allowing them to pay a lower maintenance amount or reduce the amount of time they'll be paying maintenance for, it is usually achieved with how they divide the marital estate.

STEP FIVE

Division of Assets and Debts

The final component of the marital settlement agreement and the divorce itself is determined at the same time as maintenance and child support. Step 5 in The Strategic Divorce Process is the division of marital assets and debts.

This process begins by collecting financial information through the discovery process. Each party provides statements and fills out a financial affidavit to provide as much information about their financials as possible. The parties then exchange the financial affidavits and supporting financial statements so that each party has a clear, accurate picture of the financial situation.

Once enough information has been collected, the next step is creating a spreadsheet that shows the value of each marital asset and debt so that the total value of the estate can be determined. This will help each party identify the best way to split the estate so that they are each walking away with assets and debts that amount to roughly the same value. Realistically, there are many, many ways to split the marital estate. Each asset and debt does not need to be split evenly in half; in fact, they rarely are. Instead, the goal is to ensure that each spouse walks away with a combination of assets, money, and debts that add up to roughly the same value and tax consequence, regardless of what they each retain.

Before determining how to divide the marital estate, we believe it's important to understand what is considered a marital asset or debt and what isn't.

Marital Debts

We start by determining what marital debts, if any, the couple currently has. This includes debts incurred during the marriage that either of them is responsible for paying off. There are a few different kinds of debts that are considered part of the marital estate, as well as certain debts that are not.

The first type of debt includes any debt secured by an asset, such as a mortgage, furniture, or car loan. Typically speaking, the debt is paired with an asset: if one party is going to be keeping the home, they will also be keeping any debt associated with it. The value of the home, as well as the mortgage balance, will be accounted for on the spreadsheet.

Next is credit card debt. The amount of debt present on all credit cards, regardless of whose name the cards are in, is added to the spreadsheet. Whoever's name the credit card is in will likely be the party responsible for paying off the credit card debt, but they will either receive an asset of a similar value or the other party will receive the same value of debt to keep the ultimate division of assets equitable.

Unsecured personal loans, such as a bank loan or debt consolidation loan created during the marriage, are handled like credit card debt and are usually assigned to the person whose name is on the debt. However, they will still be included on the spreadsheet and equalized and accounted for in the division of assets and debts.

Of course, not every type of debt will factor into the marital estate. For example, loans from family members with a promissory note signed by both spouses are treated the same way a loan from a bank would be. However, if a family member loans money to one of the spouses to help them with expenses related to the divorce, such as lawyer's fees, the judge often will not consider it a legitimate loan that should be considered part of the marital estate. This is because, even with a promissory note, the judge may not truly believe that a close family member will realistically expect or want the party who was loaned the money to pay them back.

Additionally, student loan debt obtained from either party earning a degree is not usually considered part of the marital estate. Instead, the debt is assumed to belong to whichever spouse received the degree. If one of the spouses took out a loan in their name to help pay for a shared child's education, this is considered a marital debt. Regardless of which spouse's name the loan is in, the person receiving the degree is the couple's child, and the courts consider the cost of college to be the responsibility of the parents. Because of this, it is assumed that both parents agreed to take on the debt. If the loan is in the child's name alone, it will often not be considered a marital debt.

Division of Assets and Debts

Marital Assets

Next, we make a list of the marital assets. A marital asset refers to anything that was acquired during the marriage. This includes obvious things, like income, bank accounts, properties, and cars, but also includes some items that people may not think of, such as businesses, retirement accounts, and stock portfolios that are started or added to during the marriage.

Additionally, any account that marital money is deposited into becomes a marital account. Even if one spouse started a large savings account prior to the marriage and continues to only have their name attached to it, it becomes a marital asset if they deposit marital income into the account during the marriage. Although there may be exceptions, this general rule is hard to disprove.

An exception to that general rule is money added to a retirement fund that was partially funded prior to marriage. It is often hard to prove what money existed prior to the marriage and what was added during the marriage, which is required to assert that a portion is non-marital. Financial institutions aren't required to keep financial records for more than 7 years, so if the marriage began 8 or more years prior to the divorce, it's unlikely that contributions made before vs. during the marriage can be traced. However, with a retirement account, if it can be traced and no money was removed during the marriage, it is possible to claim that the non-marital portion plus market gains or losses should be considered a non-marital asset.

Non-marital assets are typically properties that one person purchased prior to the marriage. Unless the spouse who owned the home prior to the marriage adds their spouse's name to the deed or refinances the house and adds their spouse's name to the mortgage, the home will stay non-marital. However, if that home is sold and a new home is purchased using money from the sale, absent a written agreement, the new home would be considered marital property. The non-marital down payment would likely be considered a gift to the marital estate unless the parties documented the intent for it to be non-marital in a signed document.

Another exception is a gift of property or money received from an inheritance or a gift to only one party during the marriage. As long as the money is kept in a separate account and is not mingled with any martial funds (like job income), it will continue to be non-marital.

While it's important to understand what is and is not considered part of the marital estate, most couples only have marital assets by the time they get divorced, either because they didn't come into their marriage with any substantial assets or because they purchased a new home and grew their estate while married.

Categorizing the Assets

After all the marital and non-marital assets and debts have been identified, the lawyers categorize the assets, which is a more complicated process. The first step is determining how each asset is classified for tax purposes.

For example, there are non-qualified assets which have no tax consequences when they are being divided because there are no tax consequences if they are converted to cash. These include checking accounts, savings accounts, cars, and the marital residence.

Qualified assets are assets that do have tax consequences. This typically includes retirement accounts, such as 401Ks, 403Bs, 457Bs, or traditional IRAs. Roth IRAs also have tax consequences, but because they are structured differently than a traditional retirement account, their classification during the division of the estate is handled differently.

Investment properties, stocks, and investment portfolios often have tax consequences as well, but what exactly those tax consequences are is often specific to each individual investment.

While these tax consequences can be avoided when dividing the marital estate because transfers between spouses do not trigger a taxable event, it's important to know what the tax consequences would be if the asset were converted to cash, as it will affect the future value of each asset. For example, if the assets are split up so that Spouse A receives all the assets with no tax consequences, totaling $500,000 of value, and Spouse B receives all the assets with tax consequences, totaling $500,000 of value, Spouse B will be responsible for paying a large amount of taxes when converting their portion of the assets to cash and will realistically end up with significantly less money than Spouse A.

Division of Assets and Debts

Once each asset and debt is classified, it's time for the next step, which is to divide them and notate the division on the asset/debt spreadsheet. Generally speaking, the value of the assets and debts are divided evenly unless the parties are negotiating with something else, like a larger maintenance payment, the length of maintenance, guilt from an infidelity during the marriage, or guilt from choosing to end the marriage. The sample asset/debt spreadsheet below shows how to divide the value of the assets and debts evenly.

CASE NAME: Book Sample
ASSET\DEBT ALLOCATION PROPOSAL - STRATEGIC DIVORCE

ORDINARY ASSETS	DATE OF VALUATION	GROSS VALUE	LIEN	NET VALUE	Husband	Wife
(JT) Marital Residence	10/30/23	$450,000	$300,000	$150,000	$0.00	$150,000
Joint Checking x3330	10/30/23	$60,000		$60,000	$60,000	$0.00
Wife's Individual Checking x4440	10/30/23	$23,916.14		$23,000	$12,500	$10,500
Husband's Individual Checking x5550	10/30/23	$38,244.68		$27,000	$27,000	$0.00
(H) 2023 Toyota	10/30/23	$42,000	$20,000	$22,000	$22,000	$0.00
(W) 2021 Honda	10/30/23	$30,000	$25,000	$5,000	$0.00	$5,000
Marital Funds spent on girlfriend - Dissipation	10/30/23	$44,000		$44,000	$44,000	$0.00
			TOTAL	$331,000	$165,500	$165,500
			%		50.00	50.00

Division of Assets and Debts

For retirement accounts like 401Ks, 403Bs, 457Bs, and IRAs, each party is entitled to half of the balance of each account. Rather than transferring half of each account to the opposite party, we determine the difference between the accounts and transfer the offset.

For example, Spouse A has $200,000 in their retirement account, and Spouse B has $100,000 in their retirement account. The total value of their retirement accounts is $300,000. Instead of each spouse transferring the other half of their account balance, Spouse A will transfer Spouse B $50,000, leaving them each with $150,000. The result is the same, but we only need to perform one transfer instead of two.

Convenience purposes aside, there is a financial benefit to this as well. A qualified domestic relations order, also known as a QDRO, is required to transfer money out of a retirement account to the other spouse, and, unfortunately, this court order is not free. By doing one transfer instead of two, only one court order is needed, so the QDRO fee only needs to be paid once.

Pensions also need to be divided if either spouse has a job that pays a pension in retirement.

Like retirement accounts, pensions are split using a QDRO. However, unlike retirement accounts, which can be valued and divided evenly based on the amount of money currently in them, pensions are a future stream of income based on the final income of the spouse receiving it, making it impossible to determine the value of the pension easily. If the marital portion of the pension is split evenly, the parties will both start to receive their portion of the pension payments after the spouse who receives the pension has retired. The marital portion of the pension is calculated based on the length of the marriage, as well as how long the person receiving the pension has been at their job.

For example, if Spouse A, a teacher, has been in their job for 23 years and was married to Spouse B for 20 years, only 20 years of the pension would be considered a marital asset. Once Spouse A retires, each spouse will begin receiving their portion of the pension monthly. Spouse B will receive 50% of the marital portion of the pension, while Spouse A will receive the rest.

Because pensions are not paid out at the time of the divorce, and the exact amount of the pension is rarely known until retirement, it is a benefit that people often forget to collect. Both spouses need to make sure to notify the courts and pension office of any change of address and keep track of the pension so they don't miss out on payments they are entitled to receive.

Stock and investment portfolios are usually pretty easy to divide evenly. In fact, most large financial service providers are able to simply split the portfolio in half. Rather than negotiate for specific stocks, the provider will split each one evenly, leaving each party with their own portfolio that closely mirrors the other party's, both in the number of shares and in their cost basis.

Similarly, savings and checking accounts are very easily divided unless an unequal split is being used to offset another asset that cannot be evenly divided, such as a house or a car.

For cars, we need to determine the equity built in the car rather than just the value. Most people have car loans, so the equity is determined by subtracting any remaining car loan amount from the fair market value of the car (which can be determined by providers like Carvana or Kelley Blue Book).

Typically, each party will keep the car they usually drive, and if there is a substantial difference in the worth of each car, savings or checking accounts can be split in a way that offsets the difference.

Division of Assets and Debts

The marital home can be one of the more complicated assets to handle simply because it is an emotionally charged one. If the couple decides to sell the home, the couple will split any money made in the sale. Much like with a car, this is determined by how much the home sells for, minus the cost of the remainder of the mortgage, realtor fees, or any other expenses incurred from selling the house. The cash from the sale will be evenly divided among the parties.

If the house is still on the market, but every other aspect of the divorce has been agreed upon, the spouses do not need to wait for the house to sell to finalize the divorce. Instead, the marital settlement agreement can clearly outline how to split any funds from the sale of the house. Often, it will also dictate how the parties will communicate with the realtor, respond to offers, and maintain the house while it is on the market.

However, if the spouses decide not to sell the house and one of them will keep it, this becomes much more complicated. First, the couple needs to determine the value of the home. They can agree to use a site like Redfin or Zillow or a current market analysis prepared by a local realtor to determine the house's worth. If they do not agree on the value, they can get an appraisal from a certified real estate appraiser to determine it. The amount remaining on the mortgage will be deducted from the appraised amount to determine how much equity has been built in the home. If the parties are unable to come to an agreement on the value of the home and, therefore, the equity in it, the court will most likely order that it be sold.

Each party is entitled to half of the home's equity in the divorce. For example, if the house is determined to be worth $500,000, and the remainder on the mortgage is $300,000, the current equity built in the home is $200,000. This means that each party is entitled to $100,000 from the home.

If one party keeps the house, they are responsible for compensating the other party for their share. How this is done, whether it be by giving the spouse a different asset of a similar value, splitting checking or savings accounts differently to make up the difference, or paying the other spouse in another way, is a negotiated issue for the parties and their attorneys to determine.

Additionally, the party keeping the house will need to refinance, removing their spouse from the mortgage and the deed within a reasonable amount of time. What is considered a reasonable amount of time is often negotiated and included in the divorce decree.

In some cases, the parties may decide to continue jointly owning the home for a few years. Typically, this is done to allow children to stay in the same home and school district they were previously in.

The couple will still need to come to an agreement that dictates how long they will have joint ownership of the house before selling it, who pays for large repairs, and how the money from the sale will be divided. There is also often a stipulation, setting conditions in case one party wants to buy the other one out of their share.

Sufficed to say, there are many different ways to divide the value of the familial home. This is because, in addition to the home typically being the largest asset they have, it is also one that people tend to be very emotionally attached to. Oftentimes, people will make emotional, rather than logical or smart, decisions when they want to stay in their residence.

They don't think of the property as an asset with high carrying costs, like ongoing mortgage payments, home insurance, and property taxes, but as their home. Without the dual income they had during the marriage, the monthly expenses may be a stretch for the person staying in the home, and they'll use a lot of money they were entitled to in the divorce or a large amount of their savings to buy their spouse out of the home.

In these cases, the spouse who kept the house often ends up needing to sell it only a few years later, losing between 6 and 10% of the home value due to closing costs and other fees. After depleting their assets to obtain or keep the house, they end up taking a large loss on the investment overall.

Although it is difficult, we urge clients to take a very close look at their finances before determining if staying in their home is a realistic and smart financial decision. In some cases, staying in the home *is* the smartest decision for one party—the mortgage payment may be extraordinarily low, and they know they won't be able to afford something similar with rising real estate prices.

Regardless, whether or not to stay in the home is a decision that should be made logically, despite the emotions that come with it.

Another asset that can create complications is a closely held business. Many people own or co-own a business, whether it be a small store, franchise, or an accounting, law, or medical practice. Regardless of the industry, before discussing any division of assets in relation to the business, the parties need to agree on what the business is worth or hire a valuator to determine the worth of the business.

Determining the value of the business is especially complicated for people who work in service industries, such as lawyers, doctors, dentists, salespeople, or accountants who may own or partially own their practice. This is because the income of the business is largely based on the work they do on an hourly basis, and their effort is not a business asset—it is their income. Therefore, the value of the business should only reflect how much it is worth when removing the spouse from the equation.

For example, if an accountant bills $200,000 annually, that does not necessarily mean the business is worth $200,000, as, without their contributions, that money would not have been earned. This means the value of a business in the service industry may be significantly lower than how much money it brings in.

However, even in service industries, there is other value in the business not based on work completed by the business owners. For example, there may be value in the client list (which could be sold to a competitor), the business phone number, patents, trademarks, the business's name, or property owned by the business.

Oftentimes, the parties are able to come to an agreement on what the business is worth. However, if they are unable to agree on the fair market value of the business, they are required to hire a business valuator. During this process, the valuator will gather financial information relevant to the business and review and critique the business's financial health, assets, liabilities, and potential future earnings. Because of how complex the process is, using a professional valuator is expensive, ranging in cost from $10,000 to $100,000, so it often isn't worthwhile unless there is a large disparity in what each party believes the business is worth or the business is a highly valued asset.

Because a business typically cannot be split evenly or at all, the party keeping the business will receive it on their side of the asset/debt spreadsheet and need to buy their spouse out of the business, usually through the division of bank accounts, or in exchange for an asset of similar value going to the other spouse on the spreadsheet.

Division of Assets and Debts

For example, if the business is worth $500,000 and there is $495,000 of equity in the home, one spouse may keep the business while the other becomes the sole owner of the family home. Alternatively, if the bank accounts have a combined total of $700,000, one spouse will keep the business, while the other will get $500,000 from the bank accounts before the remaining balance of $200,000 is divided evenly among them.

There are other large assets that may require a specialty valuator, but they come up much less frequently. This includes things like an artwork collection, an oriental rug collection, a grand piano with substantial historical or other value, sports memorabilia with significant value, or other unusual assets. Once the value of these assets has been determined, they are added to the spreadsheet.

However, any asset or item that has been given as a gift to one spouse or the other is considered non-marital and, therefore, is not factored into the asset and debt spreadsheet. A common one is an engagement or wedding ring. While they may be worth a large amount of money, they are considered gifts and are kept by the party who was given them without being accounted for on the spreadsheet.

When the division of assets is complicated, or when we are concerned somebody may be making an unwise decision that will hurt them in the long run, we often recommend that they work with an accountant or a Certified Divorce Financial Analyst, or CDFA. A CDFA is a financial analyst who is an expert on financial matters related to divorce and is familiar with any ramifications there may be for specific assets, such as tax burdens or ongoing payments.

A CDFA or an accountant can also help explain what the spouse is keeping, what they are giving up, and the effect these decisions may have in the long term. Perhaps they are giving up their share of a retirement fund in an effort to keep their house or draining their savings to keep an artwork collection without understanding how the money they are giving up will grow over time or what the financial burden of an asset they are keeping will be. A financial professional can help to ensure that the client isn't just getting what they want in the divorce but is on a good path when the divorce is over.

Unequal Split of Assets

While divorce statutes and case law dictate an equitable split of marital estates, the courts order an even split of the marital estate over 90% of the time. However, it is possible to negotiate an unequal split of assets.

Sometimes, this happens because it is impossible to evenly split the assets, like with a lucrative business that is worth more than the rest of the marital estate combined. Often, this results in the spouse receiving a larger share of the assets, making monthly payments to the other spouse to equalize the property settlement.

These payments are made in addition to monthly maintenance or child support payments. Much like maintenance and child support payments, the obligation does not end if the spouse paying them files for bankruptcy. And, unlike maintenance payments, these payments do not cease if the spouse receiving them remarries or moves in with a romantic partner.

Additionally, if there is something one party cares deeply about keeping, such as the marital home, they may negotiate an unequal split in order to keep it. A party who feels guilty over ending the marriage or an infidelity that occurred during it may be more willing to take a smaller share of the marital estate.

Should both parties agree to an unequal split, the judge will likely approve the settlement so long as it is reasonable. However, if the two parties are unable to come to an agreement and the case does go to court, the judge will almost always rule in favor of an equitable split or a split very close to 50/50. At trial, judges stick to the case law and statutes in order to reduce the risk of a trial being overturned.

Complexities during the Financial Discovery Process

There are other complexities that may occur when dividing the marital estate, and many occur during the financial discovery process.

Whether or not it is through formal discovery or informal discovery, each party is required to share their income, expenses, assets, and debts (as well as any monthly amounts paid on their debts).

At a minimum, in Illinois, the parties will provide three years of tax returns, including W-2s and 1099s, their three most recent pay stubs, and three months of bank statements. In addition, they must complete a state financial affidavit, which is signed and sworn to by each party.

If the divorce is amicable and straightforward, and both parties trust each other, this minimum discovery process may be all that is needed. However, if the divorce is not amicable, one of the parties has a reason to believe their partner is hiding something, or something suspicious comes up in the documents they produce during the informal discovery, a formal discovery may take place.

In a formal discovery, one party's lawyer will request that the other party produce documents, which are required to be produced within a certain number of days. This request will include documents as far back as 1-3 years and will include statements for bank accounts, assets, retirement accounts, credit cards, loan statements, Venmo, Apple Pay, and PayPal transaction histories, and any apps that transfer money overseas. If any of these accounts give the lawyer reason to believe that cryptocurrency has been purchased, those records are requested as well.

These statements are used to determine the value of the assets and debts for the spreadsheet. In addition, they are used to determine if there is any dissipation, which means the use of martial money for non-martial purposes after the marriage has broken down. We look for any cash removed or money spent in a way that is inconsistent with the spouse's habits during the marriage.

For example, if Spouse A withdrew $150 every week during the marriage, those continued withdrawals are not suspicious, as they are consistent with their regular behavior. However, if Spouse A suddenly started withdrawing $2,000 every week, that is inconsistent with their behavior during the marriage.

We're looking for deposits into accounts we don't know about, suspicious transfers, and unusual credit card purchases. We also want to ensure that the net amount of all paychecks is deposited in the same place they always have been.

It is important that a lawyer who knows the case and dynamics of the couple well reviews these records. Because they have detailed information about each spouse, they'll have a better idea of what is and isn't suspicious. For example, if one spouse has a BMW, a $3,000 charge at a BMW dealership makes perfect sense. However, if each spouse drives a Honda vehicle, this is something they will want to follow up on.

Oftentimes, the formal discovery won't result in anything suspicious, and the divorce will continue to move

Division of Assets and Debts

forward. Even couples who are having an amicable divorce may decide to move forward with a formal discovery simply to ensure that they understand the finances and aren't being taken advantage of.

However, if any transactions seem unusual, the lawyer will first bring it to their client's attention to see if there is a simple explanation. If not, the lawyer will then bring it to the attention of the opposing counsel and notify them that their client transferred money to a third party in extreme ways or has suspicious activity on their credit card. The lawyer will outline what the transactions are and request an explanation.

Opposing counsel often responds quickly with a reasonable explanation. Other times, they will respond that they will explain the transactions, but not immediately—this is usually a sign that money was misspent.

Money is misspent for many reasons, but the most common is on an affair partner. The markers of this are often very obvious: expensive hotel stays and dinners, jewelry or lingerie that was not given to the spouse, money transfers, or even rent or mortgage payments are all tell-tale signs that the spouse is spending money for non-marital purposes.

Another common reason is that one spouse has been anticipating the divorce for a while and began transferring money to other accounts, so it would be hidden and not factored into the divorce settlement.

Sometimes, the opposing lawyer and their client will quickly realize that they were caught misspending marital funds, admit their actions were inappropriate, and offer to put the money that was spent incorrectly on their side of the asset/debt spreadsheet, meaning their spouse will get to keep an asset of equal value or take the same amount of money out of a bank account.

The Strategic Divorce Process

For example, if Spouse A misspent $150,000, Spouse B could keep an additional $150,000 from the joint savings account before the rest of the balance of the account is evenly split.

Other times, the spouse will refuse to admit wrongdoing, and the case will go to trial. When this happens, the lawyer of the party who is alleging dissipation will file a notice of intent to claim dissipation that describes what funds they believe were spent for a non-marital purpose. It then becomes the burden of the opposing side to prove the funds are not dissipation and were, in fact, used for the marriage.

Here are a few examples of what a formal discovery may look like.

Case 1:

Spouse A's lawyer finds that Spouse B made a Zelle payment for $500 every other Friday to an account with a woman's name. Spouse A does not recognize the name. The lawyer asks opposing counsel to explain the transfers.

Spouse B's lawyer quickly notifies Spouse A's lawyer that the woman was their housekeeper's daughter, and this is how she was paid, also providing receipts. Spouse A and their lawyer are satisfied, and no further action is taken.

Case 2:

In a formal discovery, Spouse A's lawyer finds multiple suspicious credit card purchases and money transferred to unknown bank accounts going back at least four years. Included are monthly payments in excess of $5,000 and credit card charges for expensive jewelry, lavish vacations, hotel rooms, fancy dinners, and flights. In total, the amount spent is in excess of $200,000.

Division of Assets and Debts

Spouse A's lawyer informs their client that a large number of suspicious purchases and transfers were found and that they suspect the other spouse was having an affair.

Spouse A is blindsided, angry, and hurt. They want to know how long the affair went on and ask their lawyer to look back even further, but their lawyer recommends against it. In Illinois, dissipation can only be claimed for the four years prior to filing for divorce, and while Spouse A may want to know how long ago this began, it would end up costing them a significant amount of money in lawyer's fees without giving them any financial benefit.

When confronted, Spouse B's lawyer recognizes the dissipation and agrees to put the amount on Spouse B's side of the asset/debt spreadsheet, giving Spouse A a larger split of the remaining marital estate.

Case 3:

Spouse A's lawyer finds evidence of infidelity but with a very small amount of money spent on the affair. Spouse B refuses to admit wrongdoing. Spouse A is furious and wants to go to court, but their lawyer recommends that they not pursue it, as the amount of money they'd gain from proving dissipation would be worth less than the amount of money they'd spend on the attorneys pursuing it.

Case 4:

Spouse A's lawyer discovers large cash transfers to non-martial accounts and accounts in Spouse B's family member's name. The amount of money transferred is significant and took place in the two years leading up to the divorce. There were no suspicious credit card purchases, and it becomes clear that Spouse B was hoping to hide money so that it would not be divided once they divorced.

The Strategic Divorce Process

Spouse B refuses to admit any wrongdoing and goes to court. After failing to provide proof that this money was transferred for marital purposes, the judge determined that dissipation did take place and ordered Spouse A to be repaid from Spouse B's share of the marital estate. In addition, the court is likely to make Spouse B pay a larger portion of the total attorney's fees due to their conduct.

Because of how many financial records there may be to review, proving dissipation can be a long and expensive process. If one spouse suspects dissipation without any signs, the lawyer may agree to request the documents but allows the spouse to review them. If the spouse finds that it shows long-term dissipation, the lawyer may find it is worth pursuing. Alternatively, it may help negotiations and settlement, even if it is used purely as emotional leverage.

Depending on the amount of dissipation proven and the value of the estate, it may not be possible for the offending spouse to negotiate an uneven split that makes up for the money they spent inappropriately. In these cases, it will be arranged in the divorce settlement that the dissipation will be paid back over time. However, if the spouse who owes money is already paying maintenance and child support, they may not be able to realistically pay back the money immediately. In these cases, there will often be a stipulation that the spouse will pay back the money, with interest, once the maintenance period is complete. If the spouse receiving the money does remarry, the other spouse is still obligated to continue to make these payments, unlike maintenance payments.

Division of Assets and Debts

CASE NAME: Book Sample
ASSET\DEBT ALLOCATION PROPOSAL - STRATEGIC DIVORCE

ORDINARY ASSETS	DATE OF VALUATION	GROSS VALUE	LIEN	NET VALUE	Husband	Wife
(JT) Marital Residence	10/30/23	$450,000	$300,000	$150,000	$0.00	$150,000
Joint Checking x3330	10/30/23	$60,000		$60,000	$60,000	$0.00
Wife's Individual Checking x4440	10/30/23	$23,916.14		$23,000	$12,500	$10,500
Husband's Individual Checking x5550	10/30/23	$38,244.68		$27,000	$27,000	$0.00
(H) 2023 Toyota	10/30/23	$42,000	$20,000	$22,000	$22,000	$0.00
(W) 2021 Honda	10/30/23	$30,000	$25,000	$5,000	$0.00	$5,000
Marital Funds spent on girlfriend - Dissipation	10/30/23	$44,000		$44,000	$44,000	$0.00
			TOTAL	$331,000	$165,500	$165,500
			%		50.00	50.00

• • •

The Strategic Divorce Process

Dividing the marital estate can be very simple or very complex depending on the circumstances surrounding it and the mindsets of each party. The Strategic Divorce Process aims to simplify it as much as possible, as we believe it pays to be amicable, even when proving dissipation or standing up for your rights in order to lower the emotional, mental, and financial burdens of divorce.

STEP SIX

Pre-decree Litigation

Divorces may be completed quickly, especially when the parties are proceeding amicably and decisions are fairly straightforward. However, some divorces are much more complicated and become long, drawn-out processes, taking several years to finalize. Even in relatively short divorces, one party may have much greater access to marital income or assets, making it difficult for the other party to maintain their status quo, or the parties may not agree on how to handle visitation with the children before the schedule is solidified.

Because of this, parties often participate in pre-decree litigation. Pre-decree litigation establishes temporary orders for visitation, child support, maintenance, the payments of expenses and debts, and the use of marital assets before the divorce is finalized. Much like the final divorce settlement, the role of pre-decree litigation is to ensure that both parties

Pre-decree Litigation

are able to maintain their current lifestyle, as well as protect the well-being of their children if children are involved. However, unlike the final settlement, these orders are created at the judge's discretion and can be updated at any time throughout the divorce proceedings without needing to prove a change in circumstances.

These temporary rulings may be different from the future visitation schedule, division of assets, or maintenance payments. The purpose is simply to encourage both parties to engage in fair play while the divorce is happening. This protects both parties by ensuring that one spouse isn't able to take the children away from the other person or that one spouse doesn't have sole access to or control of finances.

While this process may seem like it would be reserved for contentious or long-lasting divorces, some type of pre-decree order is put in place for 50% of all divorces. These temporary orders are made fairly quickly, determined on a non-evidentiary basis, and without either party testifying or producing experts to plead their case to the court in an effort to gain the upper hand.

These orders typically fall into two categories: the Allocation Judgment and financial matters.

Many parents, especially those undergoing an amicable divorce, may not need a visitation schedule outlined. However, when divorces go on for a long time, having a set plan in place can be beneficial for everyone involved. Additionally, if the parents are unable to come to an agreement on how visitation will be handled during the divorce proceedings or are living in separate homes and need predictable schedules, a temporary order will outline it while the official visitation schedule (including decisions around holidays and vacations) is still being determined.

The Strategic Divorce Process

While temporary orders for visitation are not uncommon, it is extremely rare that a temporary order for decision-making will be put into place. Joint decision-making is standard during the divorce process unless a protective order has been granted against one of the parents, which would likely also impact the current visitation ruling.

If one parent has significantly more visitation with the children or has significantly less access to marital income to spend on the children, temporary child support can also be ordered during this time. The judge can choose to use the same equation that is used to set the final child support amount, but the court is also able to set temporary child support at their discretion and based on the needs of the children and the status quo before the divorce proceedings commenced.

Pre-decree litigation is often used to control or equalize the use of marital assets and access to marital income during the divorce. During this process, the judge will outline what the marital estate can and can't be used to pay before it is divided among the parties, such as purchasing a car or using the estate to pay their lawyer's fees.

This, of course, isn't to be confused with dividing the marital estate, which will only take place in the final divorce decree. This temporary order is simply meant to allow both parties to maintain their current lifestyle in the interim.

In the event that one of the parties has more access to marital assets than the other, the party with less access can ask for a partial pre-distribution of their share of the marital estate. This often takes place if one spouse has left the marital home and needs money in order to afford a down payment on a new residence. The judge will often allow them to borrow from their eventual share of the marital estate, allowing them to access the money they need urgently.

Pre-decree Litigation

If the parties sell a joint asset, such as the marital home, during the pre-decree litigation period, the money will typically go into escrow. Either party may ask that the judge allow them to take an advance on their settlement if they need the money before the divorce will be reasonably completed.

Parties may also use this to handle shared responsibilities, such as paying off debt on a credit card, which would otherwise be allocated once the divorce was finalized.

Additionally, if one party has less access to martial income, they may file for temporary support. If the judge agrees, the other party will be ordered to make payments before maintenance or child support is officially set.

While the judge is able to use the standard equations to calculate temporary child support or temporary maintenance, they have more flexibility during pre-decree litigation to order, on a temporary basis, whatever they think is fair. The judge may choose to exercise this power for a variety of reasons.

First, they may use this opportunity to penalize somebody who they believe is being unreasonable or unfair. If one of the parties insists on unrealistic terms, leading to an unnecessarily prolonged divorce, the judge may order that they pay a higher amount of money in temporary payments to the other party. This is done partially to penalize them and partially to incentivize them to agree to more reasonable terms so that the divorce may continue to move forward.

Alternatively, if the judge believes one person may be misrepresenting their income, the judge may set higher temporary payment amounts than the party is expecting in an effort to get them to produce accurate proof of income more quickly. It may also motivate them to gather additional evidence that the judge would consider when setting maintenance, speeding the trial, and/or settlement along.

The judge may also use this time to set expectations for the party making the temporary maintenance payments. If the party is expecting to pay a lower amount than is realistic, the pre-decree litigation period gives them time to get used to the higher payments before they become official.

If large life events happen, there may be a temporary hearing to determine how things like college tuition or large expenses for the children will be paid.

• • •

It is during the pre-decree litigation process that a notice of intent to claim dissipation may be filed, too. The final ruling will not take place until the trial, as it may have a large impact on the division of the marital estate, but the process starts during this stage of the divorce. The party claiming dissipation will begin gathering and producing evidence, as well as state their desire to be reimbursed for the dissipation, prior to the division of the marital estate.

For many parties who have less access to marital assets or marital income, the length of a divorce can be daunting. Without access to funds that allow them to maintain their current, or a similar, lifestyle, they may worry that they'll need to give in to unrealistic or unfair terms in an effort to finalize the divorce quickly. However, pre-decree litigation protects both parties and their interests until the divorce settlement is reached.

Life After Divorce

Understanding how the divorce process works, as well as the legal statutes and limitations on what a lawyer can reasonably obtain for their client, is incredibly important when facing such a life-altering event. But just as important as understanding what will happen during a divorce is planning for life after it.

When a divorce begins, it's all too easy to focus on the here and now or, worse yet, the past. Hurt feelings, anger, confusion, and pain cloud judgment, and while it is understandable, it's not in anyone's best interest to let those emotions run the show. Some people, more than anything else, want to screw over their former spouse, regardless of the cost to them. Others, desperate to get such a painful chapter behind them, hastily make decisions, often giving up more than they should.

These people often forget that there is life after divorce. And while the divorce settlement doesn't dictate what life will be like, it can have a huge role in shaping the future. Whether it's somebody paying more money in lawyer's fees than they were ever going to receive in the divorce, trading their 401k for a house that they simply couldn't afford to pay for on their own, or destroying a co-parenting relationship that could have stayed cordial, that person is negatively affected, just as much as their former spouse and kids are.

This is why, at Strategic Divorce, we believe that the goal of the divorce should always be grounded in what you want your life to look like a year or two into the future and what you need to get yourself there.

If you're looking to buy a house, what do you need financially to make that possible? If you want to spend as much time as possible with your children, how can you negotiate more than a 50/50 visitation split? Maybe you're just looking to be happy again or at peace with the decision. How can you begin to move on mentally and emotionally?

It's also important to think about what you want your relationship with your former spouse to look like, especially if you have children. How would you like to communicate with each other? How can you best work together? What kind of relationship do you want your children to have with each of you?

While we believe the answer to so many post-divorce goals starts with remaining amicable throughout the divorce process, we know that there are many hurdles that can get in the way. There may be a client who has no idea what they want, a partner who is absolutely unwilling to cooperate, or a client who doesn't understand what they may need moving forward. If we believe there is a client who needs additional

The Strategic Divorce Process

support in certain areas of the divorce, there are a number of specialists we may refer them to.

We believe these specialists can play an important role in The Strategic Divorce Process. They help clients not only get the best deal possible out of the divorce but also better envision and plan for their lives outside of it. This looks past attempting to fill short-term wants to protect overall well-being.

For clients or families who need help working through the emotional or mental aspects of a divorce, there are four types of specialists we often refer to.

First is a marriage counselor. Sometimes, we see clients come in who are unsure if they really want a divorce or seem like they may be making a rash decision. This often happens after a one-time, acute problem has occurred or from ongoing communication issues that have bubbled over when there has been no real attempt to solve them.

In these cases, we suggest that the marriage may be salvageable and refer the couple to a marriage counselor. This tends to be beneficial regardless of whether or not the couple moves forward with divorce. Many couples are able to work through the marital troubles they are having and never end up coming back to Strategic Divorce. Others find that they do, in fact, have irreconcilable differences, but after going through counseling together are in a much better place to work together and approach the divorce amicably.

Second is an individual therapist. When it becomes clear that divorce is the only way forward, we ask clients where they see themselves a year in the future, as well as what they need to get out of the divorce in order to consider it successful. Many people know right away, while others may need some time to think about it but have a pretty clear idea.

However, there are some people who are completely incapable of answering this seemingly simple question.

These people are often referred to a therapist. While the therapist will talk to them about the divorce and help them process their emotions around it, their role is actually much bigger. They are helping the client understand who they are, what their goals in life are, and helping them to gain self-confidence and self-knowledge.

This may seem like a step that is totally irrelevant in the divorce process, but it is actually very important. A client who doesn't know what they want out of the divorce or what will make them happy may have a harder time agreeing to any divorce settlement, no matter how reasonable or even favorable it may be. Their confusion will prolong the divorce, and a divorce that may have started amicably will begin to sour as their spouse loses patience. Seeing a therapist will put the spouse in a better mindset to approach their divorce logically and with the future in mind.

Additionally, couples who have children are going to be in each other's lives, whether they like it or not. Even if they create a visitation schedule that allows them to avoid seeing each other as much as possible, they will still need to communicate about large life decisions, medical needs, ongoing child-related situations, and see each other for large life events, like graduations and weddings. With that in mind, wouldn't it be better for everyone involved, especially the children, if the parents were able to get along?

Enter parenting counseling or coaching. Sessions with these experts help parents get on the same page about how to raise their children and communicate with each other. Not only does it help them make active decisions, but it sets a precedent for how decisions are made and communications are handled moving forward.

The Strategic Divorce Process

Unfortunately, the couple going through a divorce are not always the only ones who struggle. Regardless of how old they are or how well the two parents are communicating, children often have trouble making sense of the divorce and adjusting to a "new normal." In these cases, we suggest a therapist for the children, who is often able to help the child process the divorce of their parents.

Using a therapist who specializes in divorce is especially beneficial. Rather than looking at the divorce as the problem, they help the child understand that it is an unavoidable circumstance. They validate the child's feelings and help them develop the tools to work through hurt feelings and be okay despite the changes happening in their life. However, it's incredibly important that the therapist is experienced with divorce. If the therapist is not familiar with helping children through divorce, the experience may actually be detrimental to the child.

• • •

The other area we often recommend experts is handling financial matters. In many families, one spouse is responsible for handling all the financials: paying bills, tracking investments, and planning for the future. When going through a divorce, the other spouse may need help assessing what they want from the shared assets, as well as figuring out how to manage their finances independently.

Additionally, when the family has complex finances, determining what an even split will be is not always straightforward. In these cases, or in ones where we are concerned a client may be making an unwise financial decision, a Certified Divorce Financial Advisor, or CDFA, may be recommended.

A CDFA will walk the client through a financial affidavit with more assistance and explanation than a lawyer will typically provide. They'll be able to talk through complicated and unusual situations, like compensation structures that include bonuses and stock options, and help clients understand the tax implications for different ways of dividing assets.

If we're concerned that a client may be making an unwise decision, such as keeping a house that they may not be able to afford in exchange for their retirement fund, a CDFA will be able to talk them through what the impact of that will be over time, and not just in the immediate future.

On the other hand, a CDFA may be able to find a solution, helping a client keep an asset that is of great sentimental value without doing significant harm to their financial future.

In other cases, we may recommend an accountant to work alongside the CDFA, or instead of a CDFA. They can help during the divorce process by tracing money, locating or determining dissipation, and helping to document it for the courts. Additionally, in situations where income may be challenging to calculate, such as for a small business, an accountant can help illustrate and determine income.

• • •

A good divorce lawyer is the most important resource in the divorce process, and they will work tirelessly to get you a fair and reasonable settlement and, hopefully, one that prioritizes what you want from the divorce! But a great divorce lawyer looks out for your future and knows what their limitations are in helping you get there. They know when you need additional help, whether it's a therapist to help you approach the divorce with the best mindset possible, a parenting coach to help you work with your co-parent throughout your children's lives, or a financial expert who can explain the future impact of current financial decisions or analyze past financial transactions to make sure money is not missing.

A great divorce lawyer also understands how overwhelming and complicated the divorce process can be, and they strive to simplify it as much as possible.

The goal with all of these things is to keep you in the best mental and financial place so that you can approach your divorce in a way that is amicable and productive. Divorces stay amicable when both parties remain focused on the future rather than what is happening in the here and now or what happened in the past.

- Parents think about their children's well-being and avoid bad-mouthing the other parent, no matter how tempting it may be.

- Spouses don't waste time fighting over relatively unimportant items (like a blender or toaster oven) because they know they'll spend more money fighting over it than it's worth—money that could go towards their futures.

- Clients don't trade their retirement funds for a home they can't afford because they are able to assess their financial situation calmly.

Instead of seeing each other as enemies on opposing sides, the spouses understand that they need to come to a fair agreement, which will allow them both to move on relatively unscathed.

• • •

Just as there are some lawyers out there who capitalize on contentious relationships and make acrimony their business plans, there are lawyers who will attempt to take advantage of the other party's desire to be amicable. Believing that the opposing party and their lawyer will avoid court at all costs, they'll attempt to get parties to agree to terms that are so imbalanced that no judge would ever order them.

That's why it's important to have a lawyer who strives to keep each case amicable but is capable of fighting for your interests in court when need be—and who takes the time to determine what's best for you.

At Strategic Divorce, we prioritize your future by walking you through every stage of The Strategic Divorce Process. From helping you determine what is best for your children to negotiating a fair financial settlement, we fight for your interests every step of the way, helping you look forward to life after divorce.

About the Author

Michone J. Riewer has been practicing law for nearly three decades, specializing in all areas of family and matrimonial law, including custody and visitation, parental decision-making, maintenance formerly known as alimony, child support, financial issues, corporate valuations, pre- and post-nuptial agreements, adoptions, post-decree actions, and civil litigation. She also has experience in corporate law and estate planning. Her experience allows her to educate and direct each client, allowing them to successfully navigate the process and protect their future.

About the Author

After receiving her Juris Doctor from Georgia State University College of Law, Ms. Riewer moved to Illinois, where she is a member of the Illinois Bar Association, Lake County Bar Association, The Association of Women's Attorneys of Lake County, Lake County Bar Family Law Committee, the American Bar Association, and she is an advisory board member of the American Academy for Certified Financial Litigators.

Michone has received numerous honors over the years, including being recognized by Martindale-Hubbell as an AV Preeminent Attorney. She is a leading Chicago Area Divorce Lawyer, voted by her peers as one of the Nation's Top Lawyers, and recognized for Excellence in Family and Divorce Law by Lawyers of Distinction.

Michone and her team create a strategic plan for each client and then provide hands-on guidance with a commitment to exceptional service and integrity.

About Strategic Divorce

OUR FIRM AND ITS APPROACH

Strategic Divorce is a premier family law firm in Illinois that practices all aspects of family law. Our attorneys offer a broad range of expertise, from simplifying complex financial matters like high net worth assets and business advice to handling employee benefits, litigating contested custody cases, and managing post-judgment modifications. We are sensitive to the unique needs and goals of each client and provide them with the legal expertise, strategy, and support to successfully resolve their legal issues and protect themselves and their family.

THE STRATEGIC DIVORCE PROCESS

Going through a divorce or other family law matters is emotionally and financially draining, even under the best situation. Choosing the right lawyer to minimize the financial and emotional drain on you, your children, and even your soon-to-be Ex makes a challenging situation better.

The attorneys at Strategic Divorce believe divorce does not have to eviscerate your family or your finances. Our team of experienced professionals will work with you to identify your goals and then develop a strategy to accomplish them. Our clients are educated and involved in each step of the process. We help clients identify their future and then work with them to resolve their case in a way that is consistent. By employing a team approach, we ensure that every client receives individualized attention.

PROFESSIONALS COMMITTED TO EXCELLENCE

The experienced attorneys at Strategic Divorce combine their legal skills with personalized service for each client. The team approach to each case allows every detail to be handled expediently. As seasoned family law attorneys, we can advise you on what to expect in your divorce and lead you to a successful resolution.

Our attorneys are focused on the client's needs and work to negotiate divorces with the least amount of conflict. If negotiation becomes impossible, Strategic Divorce attorneys are always prepared to litigate to protect clients and their families. Our reputation for preparedness results in considerable leverage in negotiations.

FOCUSED ON YOUR NEEDS

Divorce is difficult to go through. We believe that working with your attorneys should be the easiest part. That is why we created the Strategic Divorce Process. Visit Strategicdivorce.com today for a free consultation!

INTERESTED IN CONSULTING WITH MICHONE?

SCHEDULE AN APPOINTMENT

STRATEGICDIVORCE.COM

STRATEGIC DIVORCE IS HERE TO HELP

CREATE A CLEAR PATH TO YOUR FUTURE

STRATEGICDIVORCE.COM

Michone is honored you have read her book.

Sign up for a free gift.

VISIT
STRATEGICDIVORCE.COM/WORKBOOK
AND USE THE CODE **BOOKFAN** TO
CLAIM YOUR FREE GIFT.

WE ARE ALWAYS LOOKING FOR TALENTED ATTORNEYS AND PARALEGALS

VISIT STRATEGICDIVORCE.COM/CAREER TO BEGIN PROTECTING CLIENTS AND THEIR FAMILIES' FUTURES

CONNECT WITH MICHONE AND HER TEAM

 **STRATEGICDVORCE**

 **STRATEGICDIV**

 **STRATEGIC-DIVORCE**

 **STRATEGICDVORCE**

FOLLOW THE STRATEGIC DIVORCE PROCESS

 **STRATEGICDVORCEPROCESS**

 **STRATEGICDVORCEPROCESS**

THIS BOOK IS PROTECTED INTELLECTUAL PROPERTY

The author of this book values Intellectual Property. The book you just read is protected by Instant IP™, a proprietary process, which integrates blockchain technology giving Intellectual Property "Global Protection." By creating a "Time-Stamped" smart contract that can never be tampered with or changed, we establish "First Use" that tracks back to the author.

Instant IP™ functions much like a Pre-Patent™ since it provides an immutable "First Use" of the Intellectual Property. This is achieved through our proprietary process of leveraging blockchain technology and smart contracts. As a result, proving "First Use" is simple through a global and verifiable smart contract. By protecting intellectual property with blockchain technology and smart contracts, we establish a "First to File" event.

Protected by Instant IP™

LEARN MORE AT INSTANTIP.TODAY

www.ingramcontent.com/pod-product-compliance
Lightning Source LLC
Chambersburg PA
CBHW052149070526
44585CB00017B/2035